UNLOCK THE POWER OF STORIES

CHANGE YOUR STORY, CHANGE YOUR LIFE.

TESTIMONIALS

The Art and Science of Storytelling.

People will tell you that storytelling is an art. It's a creative process and some people will tell you that they just can't do it because they are "not that creative". But these same people will sit and talk to you for hours about a subject they love and are passionate about. They often infuse this process with story after story without even noticing it.

In *Unlock the Power of Stories, Change Your Story Change Your Life*, John Cassidy-Rice and Stephen Engwell have broken down the process of storytelling to show that storytelling is not just for writers, but for everyone. They explain how it is the secret to success in not only getting what you want out of life and in communications, but also getting your message across and achieving change to have an impact on yourself, your family, business, patients or members of your team.

In this book they show that storytelling is an art and one that can be learned, it can have a process and does have real science behind it. They show what it can achieve in both those telling the story, but more importantly those listening to and losing themselves within it.

For all those in marketing, communication and sales, learning the art and science of storytelling and making it become a natural part of what they do is a must. The process is broken down into an easily readable and digestible format to allow you to practice what it preaches. They cover everything from Mirror Neurons to Pixar and what you can learn to develop your own storytelling capabilities.

As a sales, marketing and communications professional, I have no qualms about recommending this book or John Cassidy-Rice. The lessons in this book are embedded in his style of training delivery and have focused and improved my communication skills immeasurably.

Sam O'Prey
Aftermarket Sales, Behavioural Marketing and Communications Specialist.

Influence your Company's DNA.

I have seen first-hand that stories get to the heart of the matter in business. They are most effective when colleagues and customers are given the freedom to share and listen to stories, good and bad, in an open and trusted environment. Only if these stories are listened to and acted upon do they start to become part of a company's DNA. This then informs its cultural make up and becomes the true heartbeat of the organisation, their reason for being and the catalyst for positive change and reinforcement. As a consequence the company will stand out from the crowd; this book will start you on your journey to be able to do just this.

Jason Sharpe
www.Vallum.co.uk

Stories to Shape the World.

Storytelling, why bother? In this world of efficiency, who has time, right? In his book *Unlock the Power of Stories, Change Your Story Change Your Life,* John Cassidy-Rice demonstrates precisely why those who don't bother, are missing a vital trick to better engage with everyone they connect with. This is something our ancestors have known for centuries, millennia even. Stories don't just change people, they can shape the world. Bringing together theory from psychology, economics and Neuro Linguistic Programming, John illustrates some of the science and history behind storytelling with accessible examples ranging all the way from *Ancient Chinese Military Strategy*, though *Star Wars* all the way to *Finding Nemo* – all bound by the compelling rationale for investing a little time up-front in structuring your tale. Why? Because stories don't just change people, they can shape the world. The good news that this book reminds us of is that everyone is a born storyteller, it's just that some of us don't realise it, have forgotten, or don't think we have time. Make time and you too can shape the world. Of course, if you are unsure where to start in shaping the world, start here with this book – like any good book, start at the beginning.

Graham Curtis-Coles

Stories that create the most memorable courses and presentations.

Surely stories have no role in such a data-driven company as mine? So really, what practical use could this book be? However, the book reminded me that some of the courses and presentations that you remember the most now are not the ones packed with data, but the ones that use wonderful metaphors and stories Extracting the practical techniques from the book and applying a few minutes of thought allowed me to see that you can find applications for stories, and in turn start to develop the same level of impact that the metaphors and stories you remember had, even in a data-driven company. The very thought of telling 'stories' puts me off as I'm no orator, however, I am open to learning. John's words were enough to have me create a few stories off the back of the book by using simple metaphors and one of the story structures provided – maybe not *Alice in Wonderland,* but impressive nonetheless. It's all good practical stuff that you can use at work to create impact.

Mike Thomlinson

Transforming stories worth listening to.

Stories transform lives. You know this. You may not know you know it, but you do. John Cassidy-Rice knows it too. I know he knows it because he has been telling me stories since I first met him in 2009.

John's stories, in part, helped me change my stories and beliefs to change my life. Now John is sharing what he knows with you. It'll be worth your while to listen.

Andrew Chad

Going down the rabbit hole.

Reading John Cassidy Rice's new book on Storytelling is a little like talking to John himself. One minute the narrative is helping you understand the scientific reason why stories are so powerful, the next you're being led deep into a rabbit hole of ideas, suggestions and artful ⬛⬛⬛⬛⬛⬛⬛ myself on more than one o⬛⬛⬛⬛⬛⬛⬛ between what I was read⬛⬛⬛⬛⬛⬛⬛ up into my mind as I re⬛⬛⬛⬛⬛⬛⬛ packed full of provocat⬛⬛⬛⬛⬛⬛⬛ second, third and subse⬛⬛⬛⬛⬛⬛⬛ the power of the book co⬛⬛⬛⬛⬛⬛⬛

Graham David

COPYRIGHT AND LEGAL INFORMATION

General Information
Copyright © 2017 by John Cassidy-Rice. All rights reserved.

No part of this publication may be reproduced or transmitted in any form or by any means, mechanical or electronic, including photocopying and recording, or by any information storage and retrieval system, without written permission from the publisher.

Publisher: Training Excellence Ltd
www.nlpcourses.com

Legal Information
While they have made every effort to verify the information provided in this publication, neither the author nor the publisher assumes any responsibility for errors in, omissions from or different interpretation of the subject matter.

The information herein may be subject to varying laws, regulations and practices in different areas, states and countries. The purchaser or reader assumes all responsibility for use of the information. The publication is not intended as a source of legal or accounting advice and, where appropriate, the advice of a suitably qualified professional should be sought. The author and publisher shall in no event be held liable to any party for any damages arising directly or indirectly from any use of this material. Any perceived slight of specific people or organizations is unintentional.

Every effort has been made to accurately represent this product and its potential and there is no guarantee that you will earn any money using these techniques and ideas. Any links to other websites are for information only and are not warranted for content, performance, accuracy or any other implied or explicit purpose.

Table of Contents

UNLOCK THE POWER OF STORIES 1
TESTIMONIALS 2
INTRODUCTION 9
    JOHN'S STORY 11
    STEPHEN'S STORY 18
RABBITS, BELIEFS, INFLUENCE, COMMUNICATION, PIGS AND CHILD DEVELOPMENT 23
KING ARTHUR, MERLIN, FREUD AND THE MOVIES. 38
THE HERO'S JOURNEY, UGLY OGRES, DONKEYS AND JEDI KNIGHTS. 49
MIRROR NEURONS, MONKEYS, ISOMORPHIC METAPHORS, PIXAR AND FISH. 67
STORYTELLING ….BUT WHERE TO START? 83
STORIES FOR OTHER PEOPLE. 112
HOW TO USE THIS BOOK. 132
BIOGRAPHIES: 136
    JOHN CASSIDY-RICE 136
    STEPHEN ENGWELL 137
APPENDIX 138

INTRODUCTION

Some of the fondest memories of my dad were when he read bedtime stories to me and my brother. Even though he passed away many years ago, those stories still connect me to my father and those precious moments we had together.

As a father myself now, I will go out of my way to ensure I regularly read to my children as I now realise that this simple act is a means of creating healthy adults. The origin of storytelling is lost in the mists of time but can be traced to myths, legends, fairy tales and fables etc. Parents have appreciated the value of storytelling for some time, but it is only now that scientists are acknowledging the power of stories.

We as humans are story making beings. The stories you tell yourself and others create your beliefs, values and thoughts; these ultimately manifest as your results and in life. These can be negative or positive and so by changing the story it is possible to change the belief for the better. For example, heading for a job interview you may find yourself saying, "I'm so nervous. I'm going to fail this". Or perhaps, "I've prepared so well that I'm going to give this my best shot". These 'stories' will affect the outcome.

As we delve deep into this book we will discover how stories have the ability to change us as we realise we are tapping into one of the most powerful communication tools available; one that has stood the test of time.

It is often said that, "With great power comes great responsibility" (see Appendix *). In the right hands the knowledge in this book has the potential to transform the world for good.

You can expect many results from reading this book. Fundamentally, you will begin to understand how the brain processes stories and consequently be able to shape and bend realities. Wow that's quite a striking claim, so do you doubt me? Let's just pause to reflect and consider why some of the greatest marketeers, sales people and leaders in their specialist fields have all studied the art of storytelling. Let me tell you, if you think you know of a leader who does not tell stories, then they are not likely to be a particularly great leader. Let's put this in the context of my remark about 'bending realities' with an example.

Stories prepare us for change when the time is right. Let's consider Barack Obama, the African American politician who served as the 44th President of the United States from 2009 to 2017. Yes, the 44th president and the first black president. He took up the position based on a high percentage of eligible voters that shattered previous records. This story in itself represented a signal for significant change. But it was the exploration of the "idea" of a black president in novels, movies and television, both before and after the election of Barack Obama that may have accustomed Americans to accept a black man as president. Actor Dennis Haysbert, who played a black president on the first series of the hit show *24* back in 2001 said, the portrayal "may have opened the eyes, the minds and the hearts of people because the character was so well liked". You may now begin to understand how stories can influence perception and start to bend reality.

The art of constructing stories is being lost. It gets worse when people believe and say that they are not a natural storyteller; this immediately passes that power to someone else to shape their minds, their thinking and eventually lose their voice. Fortunately this book will address this issue. Anybody is perfectly able to construct and tell stories. The frameworks provided will be a great help. Examples of effective frameworks span those used by the filmmaker George Lucas in *Star Wars* to those used by Pixar in the movie *Finding Nemo* ….from the heavens to the depths of the ocean.

JOHN'S STORY

My own personal story was shaped from the age of seven. It was discovered that I was dyslexic; ironically not just a difficult word to pronounce, but also to try and spell! In addition to this my parents struggled financially and found it difficult to make ends meet. Mum made my clothes and cut my hair using the stylish 'basin cut' method. Birthday and

Christmas presents were homemade. As an adult now I understand and appreciate the efforts that were made, but as a kid at the time I really wanted what other kids had, the bionic 'Six Million Dollar Man' action figure.

It wasn't until my twenties that I started to discover the power of storytelling and how the stories I was telling myself affected my life. As a result of my childhood I was constantly running two negative stories in my head. The first I would tell myself, "You're dyslexic, worthless and stupid….who would want to date me? Who would want to hire me?" This would manifest itself as shyness, low self-esteem and learning issues. The second was linked to poverty with: "I'll never make anything of myself". I suffered long periods of unemployment and any jobs I did secure were based on minimum wage. This included taking sewage waste samples and delivering them to the lab for analysis – quite literally a breath-taking experience. All this only served to compound my already low self-esteem. So what did I do to turn this around? I started to change the stories I was telling myself.

This transformation was not immediate and it took time and much effort on my part. I began to question what it meant to be dyslexic and reframed this by exploring its benefits. It all started with a story being told by Sir Richard Branson, a dyslexic himself. He spoke about the condition in an interview. It's a hazy recollection, but I do remember him mentioning that 65% of all self-made millionaires at that time were dyslexic. I can't be sure if this was entirely true, but it was such a powerful remark that impacted on me and so it became the new story I would tell myself.

As I began to tell myself the new story I focused on the benefits of dyslexia to open up new worlds for me. I started to read biographies of successful people who shared this condition and I was even lucky enough to meet some of them. They became role models that would reaffirm the idea that people with dyslexia were brilliant and this helped to unlock my potential.

This new evolving positive state of mind took several years to cultivate and grew in my behaviour and allowed me to eventually develop a flourishing career. I now appreciate the benefits of dyslexia and feel truly blessed. I enjoy a wonderful life with my wife, five children and my first grandson. I also travel the world on business and feel humbled and proud to have served thousands of people. My training company is now one of many companies I run and they all bring me and others great joy.

I want to return to a point I mentioned above and the misunderstanding that some people feel they cannot tell stories. This is just a misperception and I want to explode some myths around storytelling. I want to reassure you that you can and you do tell stories. For example, if asked the simple question "What did you do last week?" the response might be: "Well I went to the flower show. It was a lovely warm day, the sun was shining as we visited the show gardens and I even bought some unusual plants and seeds for our own garden". This is a form of story that flows quite naturally. Maybe not the most riveting of stories, but with a little thought and using the techniques revealed in this book, you will be able to cultivate a blossoming and life changing story.

Another myth about stories relates to the business world. I've often heard, "I'm a business woman and as such we don't tell stories". Well that's just crazy and quite untrue. Most of the biggest companies in the world utilise stories. It has been said that if you can't properly convey a story then your products are not going to appeal to your audience. You'll therefore find stories incorporated into all forms of company content such as blogs, e-books, articles and the "About us" page on websites.

These all serve to engage and captivate the audience leaving them wanting more, however, some company stories can be more effective than others. This is particularly well demonstrated by the types of stories that the technology company Apple have been telling their audiences. Their approach was determined and effectively explained by Simon Sinek in a 'Ted Talks' video clip, widely available on the internet, using a 'What, How and Why' model. For communication and marketing Sinek explains how most companies tend to follow the sequence: 'What' (all companies know what they do); 'How' (some know-how and provide a differentiating value proposition/proprietary process/unique selling point); 'Why' (few know why they do what they do in terms of their purpose). However, the more inspired organisations communicate this sequence in reverse.

If Apple were like everyone else their marketing message would follow the standard sequence and might be, "We make great computers, they're beautifully designed, simple to use and are user-friendly. Wanna buy one?" But their story is quite different and their actual approach is this sequence *in reverse*: "Everything we do we believe in challenging the status quo, we believe in thinking differently. The way we challenge the status quo is to design computers that are beautifully designed, are simple to use and are user-friendly. We just happen to make great computers, wanna buy one?" That's it; you're ready to buy a computer from Apple…..or even a phone, a tablet, a laptop or a watch etc. *People don't buy what you do; people buy why you do it.* The goal is to do business with people who believe what you believe. This formula has put them ahead of their competitors and it's quite an impressive marketing story.

Apple has produced many stories about their business. According to the biography of Steve Jobs, the company name 'Apple' was conceived by him after returning from an apple farm. Apparently he thought the name sounded "fun, spirited and not intimidating". The name may have also benefitted by beginning with an 'A', which meant it could be found nearer to the top of any listings. I recently read an article about the electronic commerce and cloud computing company Amazon. I discovered that whenever an employee goes into a sales meeting they must bring with them a story to explain how the customer will be using a proposed new product or service. It's interesting that the company name also begins with the letter 'A'.

Companies rely on their customers to tell stories about them such as testimonials and general feedback that can be shared. Living in the UK we may not be so familiar with a company called Zappos, an online shoe and clothing shop. I have been more aware of them because many authors and people write stories about their amazing customer service. Employees were encouraged to go above and beyond traditional customer service. So great was their success that Amazon eventually acquired it in an all stock deal worth over $1b. That's a great story and immediately moved that company from 'Z' to 'A'.

If you would like just moderate success, then don't bother telling stories. But if you'd like to become a world-class business then tell stories.

Of course this can apply to all walks of life, even a scientist. But surely a scientist must focus purely on facts? I was reading an article in 'The New Scientist' about scientific discoveries. Towards the end of the various accumulative successes it concluded that: "what we really have here is a list of significant achievements that amounts to a fascinating story, one told by a particularly good storyteller".

Over the last 10 years we have seen an upsurge in the publication of scientific books. They have tended to share a common characteristic in that efforts have been made to ensure the content is much more accessible and understandable; they have brought science alive and made it more interesting using stories to reflect basic principles. I have heard that sales for the general public have now exceeded those for university study. Just pause to consider the success of the popular physicist Professor Brian Cox and his series of TV shows 'The Wonders of....' These have provided fascinating stories on 'The Wonders of The Universe' and 'The Wonders of Life'; topics that may have once been considered to be tedious and dull have been brought to life with intrigue. The names of the most influential scientists have become mainstream because of the stories told about them, e.g. Albert Einstein, Richard Feynman and Stephen Hawkins to name but a few.

As we go forward together in this book, our goal is to reclaim our right as individuals to tell stories and, at the same time, to reveal what it means to be human. Our quest awaits - grab your sword and your shield and be ready to defend your right to tell stories and strike out to achieve change.

John Cassidy-Rice

STEPHEN'S STORY

My own personal story was shaped from around the age of nine. I grew up in Peckham, South London and lived just off the Old Kent Road in a big old house, just 2 doors down from my primary school, Camelot. My parents came from humble beginnings. My father was a postman working in a sorting office and my mother worked in the rag trade; both worked hard to support the family. Like most people of those times their incomes were relatively low, but they always aimed to ensure I had the fundamental things I needed and wanted. I loved my first big bicycle without stabilisers and those strap on roller skates. Mum was certainly the influential driving force.

Throughout my life I have been fortunate to have mentors to inspire me and invariably these people had some influence on my education. Of course I had no knowledge of the role of a 'mentor' then and you'll learn the importance of these in 'The Hero's Journey' of this book. The first mentor I can recollect was my primary school teacher, Mr Todd. At such a young age I suspect I had no true realisation of the importance of education and little thought for the future. This man showed great interest in me and became a strong influence, so much so that I developed a deep respect for him and I wanted to do well in his classes.

Looking back I realise I how much I enjoyed stories of fantasy and escapism. I can visualise even now sitting before a teacher and being spellbound as she turned the pages of *Aesop's Fables* and *Grimm's Fairy Tales*. However, Mr Todd told what he believed to be one of the greatest stories ever written. He never actually mentioned the name of the story, but I remember sitting at an old wooden, ink-stained desk being transfixed by his weekly sharing of instalments of a tale about someone called 'Jean Valjean'. He never once read direct from a book, but verbally told the story in a magical fashion with gestures, a gentle tone and the most amazing chalk drawings on the blackboard. The story was packed full of morals, principles and it arguably fits one of the key frameworks given in this book. It wasn't until much later in life that I realised he was recounting the great Victor Hugo novel, *Les Misérables*.

One day Mr Todd called all the classroom children to his desk individually to recite the Times Tables in ascending order from two to twelve. He had previously issued us all with cards detailing the multiplication to learn. This matter has become seared into my memory as I failed dreadfully at this task and felt I had let him down. I think I stalled during the three times table and I guess I didn't understand what I needed to do to in order to learn. I remember being particularly envious of my friend who successfully completed them all in one session and even went on to conclude with the thirteen times table.

Why couldn't I do this? At such a tender age I began telling myself the story that I was a failure, that I was hopeless and that I'd never progress. But this mentor's influence was so strong that I decided to change the story and take some control of the situation. In tears after school I explained the situation to my Mum and asked for her help. My parents' education hadn't been particularly great, but Mum wanted to help and let me regularly practice the Times Tables with her. Through persistence, determination and running a new story that 'I can do this'; I gradually escalated to cover all the Times Tables. I cannot claim that the learning was easy at the time, but this was my baptism of fire and I discovered the importance of having to make an extra effort to achieve something you really want. I also learned that is it's ok to ask for help rather than flounder. My ability to learn improved dramatically by the end of primary school and I remember proudly tackling something called 'English comprehension'.

So I began to change the story and change my belief that learning and progressing was quite possible. Thereafter I worked hard at school and generally throughout my working life, often striving for the best and aiming for a certain level of perfection. Those who know me well know that I pay great attention to detail to set and follow incremental goals. Some may not consider perfection to be particularly healthy, but for me: "Shoot for the moon. Even if you miss, you'll land among the stars." *(Norman Vincent Peale, 1898-1993).* The difference between being ordinary and extraordinary is doing that little bit extra. Some people find this to be a little cliché, but remember this when you hear about *The Three Little Pigs* later in this book and why one was able to succeed.

I then followed a consistent and successful career with many more mentors in local government. I worked in Human Resources and became a Chartered Fellow of the Chartered Institute of Personnel and Development (CIPD) to specialise in Learning & Organisational Development. I enjoyed coaching and helping others wherever I could. I didn't consider this to be too bad for the cockney kid who grew up off the Old Kent Road. Local government financial constraints began to worsen and redundancy caught up with me in 2012. This can be a traumatic time for anyone in this situation and can impact on personal confidence. However, this was a milestone and I decided to tell myself yet another new story.

I knew I wanted to do something different, to continue helping others and to pursue something that had been intriguing me. I wanted to study this thing called 'NLP' (Neuro Linguistic Programming) and was so fortunate to discover and be trained by yet another respected mentor. This was of course John and I was so moved by his personal story, something he also often shared in his training classes. Anything is possible. "But I'm too old to learn something new", is one of the most unnecessary and self-sabotaging comments I hear people say. It's just not true, but it does require commitment. Change the story, challenge yourself, change that belief and be amazed. Am I crazy or mad to suggest this? *"Dreams are often most profound when they seem the most crazy"* - *Sigmund Freud.*

When I saw the extreme results I was achieving with NLP, I wanted more. I soon qualified as an NLP Master Practitioner, trained in Hypnosis and suddenly found myself being sought for increasing amounts of written work. From our respective stories, feedback and outcomes achieved, both John and I are often regarded as 'heroes' who have undergone transformative journeys - you'll understand more of this from the storytelling frameworks given in this book. It has been a joy to work together in producing this book, to better understand why we all behave the way we do and that change is possible.

"But I don't want to go among mad people," Alice remarked.
"Oh, you can't help that," said the Cat: "we're all mad here. I'm mad. You're mad".
"How do you know I'm mad?" said Alice.
"You must be," said the Cat, "or you wouldn't have come here."
― Lewis Carroll, Alice in Wonderland

Let's go down the rabbit hole.......

Stephen Engwell

CHAPTER 1

RABBITS, BELIEFS, INFLUENCE, COMMUNICATION, PIGS AND CHILD DEVELOPMENT
- THE POWER OF STORIES

In this opening chapter we are going to explore contrasting topics. What could possibly link rabbits, beliefs, influence, communication, pigs and child development? It's intriguing and as you read further you will discover that there is a meaningful association that will join these together in a cohesive fashion using a timeless process; one that can positively persuade and help to transform us all. That's storytelling.

The importance of communication.

Stories have played an important part throughout history and today we can communicate in more innovative ways than ever before. Immediate phone calls, texts, emails and the use of many forms of social media have all overtaken semaphore and the hand written letter. The internet has replaced the courier pigeon. Yet despite all this, miscommunication is rife in our society today. There's a mantra, 'be more factual and keep to the facts'. The hectic and busy lifestyles of today, combined with our growing sense of self-importance, are eroding the time available to devote to stories. People seem to forget that the act of firing off an email doesn't necessarily mean an idea has been properly communicated. Thoughts and intentions may often swirl around in our heads, but just how good are we at conveying their meaning?

Have you considered those conversations you occasionally have with yourself; perhaps thoughts about what you want to achieve or improve in life? The list of aspirations can be endless, e.g. to be:

* a better teacher
* a more supportive parent
* able to inspire a team
* a lover
* a trainer or public speaker
* more effective in marketing and sales etc.

These are all worthy objectives and you are only constrained by the limits of your imagination. In order to allow any one of these to become reality, it's important to understand how the brain processes information to improve our communication at every level.

A rabbit in the headlights.

Let's explore communication from the perspective of storytelling. There have been lots of theories proposing that we are storytelling creatures and how the brain likes to naturally process information. This may explain why certain charismatic people, such as therapists, coaches, teachers, world leaders and business owners, can make such a big difference by connecting at multiple levels through their storytelling.

Let me introduce you to Dr Roger Sperry (1913–1994). He was a successful neuropsychologist and neurobiologist who, together with his colleagues, won the 1981 Nobel Prize in Physiology and Medicine for his work with split-brain research. His focus was the functional specialism of the cerebral hemispheres and discovered that the brain was actually made up of two parts, and that they processed information in different ways. We now know that the left hemisphere of the brain focuses on processing information in an analytical and logical way; it reduces things down to its component parts and puts them together to form the whole. However, the right brain processes information based on the big picture and looks for meaning and processes the emotions. It is intuitive and will go pattern hunting to look for consistent themes occurring.

The great thing about storytelling is that the mere process seems to stimulate *both* the left brain, which is the language processing, *as well as* the right brain intuition to create a much deeper meaning and understanding. Therefore, this connection of the two hemispheres can be a very powerful method of communication during storytelling.

We tend to think in stories and storytelling naturally stimulates the brain to fill in gaps where there may be missing information. I'll demonstrate this with just three little words. Consider the following carefully:

Rabbit – Road – Car

Most human brains look for a connection between the isolated words. The brain will start to make associations based on what it already knows. Then, for the remainder it will fill in enough of the missing parts to create a meaningful story. Of course, different people can interpret the meaning in differently ways. From just those three words you would have created some meaning, your own story.

Therefore, in some stories poor Mr. Bunny gets flattened.

However, conversely your brain may have chosen to let him see the car coming and to react. Your brain may have Mr. Bunny standing up on his hind legs and facing the oncoming car. You may have visualised him lifting up his front paws - first the left one, then the right to block out the dazzling headlight beams before he ducked with seconds to spare…thinking, "I hope this isn't a Reliant Robin!" Your brain's 'gap filling' then has Mr. Bunny hopping home and telling an exciting story. He's a hero who stared in the face of danger and yet lived to tell the tale. For other people, their brains may not have realised it was even dark.

I introduced the ludicrous idea of a rabbit spinning around and blocking out the headlights before ducking to offer a different outcome. The strange thing is that this idea now becomes part of the pattern of thoughts that you will now run, known as a *schema*. The next time you hear the succession of words 'rabbit', 'car' and 'road', your brain will run both ideas, i.e. both 'stories'.

Yes the first story outcome is likely to be the stronger. It's the sort of story you may have had kicking around your head for a while and so it has become the stronger story. However, although the second story may not have been quite so strong, if you repeat this frequently in your mind you will find that it will become the more dominant. This explains why repetition can be effective as it can reinforce new ideas.

Repetition. Repetition.

New 'ideas' can be synonymous with what we call 'stories'. Beliefs are the stories we tell ourselves to prove that we are right. If you change the story around your beliefs then you can change your beliefs. One of the ways of doing this would be to continuously repeat the new story over and over to yourself, and to anyone who would listen, and you will be creating your own new realities. Repetition and storytelling are also effective when creating realities in other people.

Where might we see evidence of this? Let's take marketing. Just consider advertisements that are played over and over again as they weave in a powerful story. That then becomes 'sticky' as you get what is known as 'top-of-mind awareness'

(TOMA) as the brand or product then becomes first in the customer's mind. If I were to ask you to imagine a short, rotund man with a curly moustache, wearing a black opera suit and singing "Go Compare"....what might that evoke in you?

This isn't a new concept and can be traced back to Aristotle and is often used in public speaking and presentations to help the audience remember. The approach is often used to help people build a case for their ideas. Tell them what you are going to tell them. Tell them. Tell them what you've just told them. You then have repetition of the message, but the magic happens when you also weave in a great story.

There was once a group of scientists who wanted to find out what it meant to be human. So they gathered a wealth of data and input this to the most powerful computer they could find and set it to process the information. The computer processed the data for days until eventually the machine came to a halt with a 'ping' to indicate the answer was ready. Everybody crowded around ready to discover the answer to what it meant to be human. The computer's first line of output text read….. "Let me tell you a story".

Children's stories.

It's possible to track the stages of healthy human development through storytelling and this starts during early childhood. Children go through various stages of storytelling during their formative years and it's important for parents and guardians to 'scaffold the story', i.e. build content within the story.

Stories often start off with just one word. For example, a toddler may waddle up to its parents in a room and gaze up at them to utter the single word, "Bang!" Parents will instinctively take this as a warning, jump up and scream, "Oh no….the TV set!" They rush into the adjoining room to discover the TV smashed in pieces on the floor.

As children start to age and move from two years, to three and then to four years, you will find that they develop a tendency to mutter in bed. As parents put them to bed children can be heard whispering random comments to themselves like: "So Nana came over today. I like Nana, she gives me big kisses and she always gives me cuddles. I think Nana is sweet and she is daddy's mummy". The child is actually recalling and sorting through all the memories and thoughts collected throughout the day, and it's important to allow the child time to sift through all their information.

From about the age of five to seven, as the child grows older, you will begin to hear types of 'black and white' storytelling involving more clearly defined and often opposing principles or issues, e.g. "Oh, Suzy pushed Jenny over. We don't like Suzy anymore because she made Jenny cry".

Then we progress into an older age range. It's usually around eight and above for girls, slightly delayed in boys, when we find much more complex stories: "So Jenny likes Tony, but Tony doesn't like Jenny, but we think they would make a nice couple and that they could start to go out together". You can see how stories help us to understand and track where a child is in their stage of natural human development.

The benefits of stories.

(i) Stories with morals.
Then we have universal stories that teach us valuable lessons. Let's take the example of the story of *The Little Three Pigs*. What is the meaning behind this story that has been so enduring? Well it's a poignant story about work ethic. Cast your mind back to remember that it was all about the pigs building houses of different materials. The first little pig built a house from straw and made very little effort. The second little pig made a greater attempt and built the house from sticks. It was the third little pig that was more mindful of predators and safety, so decided to expend more time and effort to work hard to build a sturdy structure out of bricks. You'll know that the first two pigs' houses suffered the wrath of The Big Bad Wolf, whereas the third pig's house survived. You can see that this simple but lasting story carries the morals about the value of making a real effort upfront, to consider the implications of what you're doing and ultimately being rewarded.

What we start to discover here is that storytelling is at the heart of influence, communication, being charismatic and being able to make a difference in the world as a therapist, coach or business owner etc. Stories can underpin a healthy individual and allow us to track the development of children as they grow. Stories form the basis of our beliefs - change the story surrounding the beliefs we tell ourselves and our lives starts to change.

(ii) Metaphors.
Let's quickly now consider 'cognitive linguistics', i.e. that language is an instrument for organising, processing and conveying information. It also proposes that all words are metaphors. For example the English language has the metaphors for 'up' being good and 'down' being bad. We hear phrases like: 'He was an upbeat guy', 'things are looking up' and 'things are coming up roses'. On the other hand, he was a 'down beat guy', 'he was down on his luck' and so 'really scraping the bottom of the barrel now'. The delicate interwoven tapestry of a good story can be quite a compelling yarn. More detail about metaphors will follow.

(iii) Goal setting.
Storytelling forms the foundation for goal setting. I have explored goal setting for many years now. I have noticed that some people can set a goal and seem to achieve it with minimal effort, while others go through all the right processes, develop plans, visualise the outcome etc. only to struggle to achieve their goals. What could be holding them back? Well, it's my opinion that people who achieve their goals with elegance and ease simply

tell themselves a much better story, one that fires their imagination.

(iv) Accelerated learning.
Storytelling can also provide accelerated learning and great teachers are wonderful story tellers. Let's take a couple of interesting examples:

(a) Example of a simplistic lesson in electricity:
Student: "What is electricity like as it flows through the wires?"
Teacher: "Well it's just like water flowing through pipes".
Student: "Is it? I've seen water flow through pipes, is it very similar?"
Teacher: "Well not precisely, that was just a quick and easily analogy to help you broadly understand what is happening".
Student: "Hmm, that's helpful. Let's make it a little trickier now. So what does a resistor do?"
Teacher: "Ok, you have the water continuously flowing through the pipes, but then you block one end. The water continues to flow in and pressure builds up. By making a small hole in the blocked end will allow some of the water to escape and squirt out to ease the pressure. You then begin to control the flow rate of the water".
Student: "Oh yes that sounds plausible, I understand how that could work".

You can see how a very simple story could expedite learning and understanding. However, storytelling this powerful can also have its drawbacks.

(b) Example of a simplistic lesson in physics:
Student: "What's it like inside an atom?"
Teacher: "Well that's like our universe".
This broad statement may then start to create possible erroneous thoughts for a student.
Student: "So the Nucleus becomes the sun and the electrons that go around the outside are the planets".

So although it's possible to appreciate a metaphor like that to help understand something complex very quickly, it's possible to also take on a number of presuppositions associated with that metaphor which may not be correct. In this example the sun is at the centre and that's ok as 'the Nucleus'. However, the Electrons can take on the presupposition by some that the planets are in a fixed orbit, but this is not the case as they whizz about in a random fashion.

This demonstrates how stories can affect our beliefs, because they create presuppositions that our minds will hold to be true. It's therefore important to be careful of the stories and metaphors we use in any discipline.

There is a metaphor taken from Sun Tzu's *The Art of War*, written back in the second century BC that links 'sales' to the 'battlefield'. Sun Tzu was a high-ranking general in the Chinese military and wrote one of the most influential strategic and tactical military books in history, but there is an analogy where sales reps are likened to sales warriors. The book is often used as part of sales training.

When you consider the core subject here, is the art of '*war*' really the right type of metaphor to be used when looking to make a sale? Let's step back and analyse this for a second. In this context of war/selling who would be considered the enemy? Well this would be the customer. Therefore who are you planning to attack and who is going to get injured? Well that would be the customer. I have mentioned above how presuppositions can easily become attached to a metaphor, so in this instance is this likely to be the best metaphor to use to achieve a sale?

Many years ago, long before supermarkets and the local stores existed, villages were often isolated and would eagerly await a visit from a travelling salesperson who could supply goods that weren't readily available. Using a very entertaining style, often in the form of a show, they were able to provide specialist wares. These could be varied items such as herbs and spices as well as services to fix pots and selling plants etc. The metaphor used here in storytelling is much more pleasant and is based on the premise of: 'How can I serve you?' For me this is an altogether better approach than metaphorically linking the customer with warfare.

Recapping the plot so far.

What have we learned in this chapter?

* The brain can process information to improve communication at every level.

* We rescued a rabbit from being run over and he is now a hero.

* Storytelling stimulates both the left brain (language processing) as well as the right brain (intuition) to create a much deeper meaning and understanding.

* Beliefs are stories we tell ourselves. Change the story, change the belief.

* Never leave young children alone in a room with your expensive 52inch, 4k Ultra HD, curved screen smart TV.

* Repetition is one of the keys for changing our beliefs, as well as changing the stories we tell about ourselves and to other people.

* It is possible to track the stages of healthy human development through storytelling. Allow and encourage children to tell their own stories. As teachers/parents/guardians, the quality of the stories we tell children during their development will create significant life lessons for them.

* Metaphorical storytelling can accelerate our learning, but be mindful of the presuppositions and how they can sometimes create misunderstanding and confuse. Tell the right story, i.e. in sales is the metaphor of 'warfare' more effective than 'How can I serve you?'

* Never build a house made out of straw - wise to go for the brick option. Take your time and make a greater effort to achieve your longer-term reward.

* We tend to more readily engage when we're having some fun. We enjoy a greater flow and can learn more quickly when stories contain elements of humour.

* Stories are very powerful methods of communication and marketing. The more inspirational organisations realise that *people don't buy what you do; people buy why you do it.*

You may now be starting to realise how powerful and effective storytelling can be. This advanced communication skill can affect all of us all on multiple levels and that this is a skill worth mastering. In the forthcoming chapters we will explore this topic in much more detail. I will explain how to create dynamic, interesting and riveting stories that capture and hold attention such that it can influence and change people's lives. In short, storytelling can achieve positive transformation and help individuals to accomplish their wildest dreams. That's pretty powerful!

As the first chapter draws to a close we have covered a great deal. There is much more learning to follow in the ensuing chapters as we examine the real skills involved in storytelling.

CHAPTER 2

KING ARTHUR, MERLIN, FREUD AND THE MOVIES.
- THE MASTER SKILL OF STORYTELLING.

To continue the theme of what might be considered 'unusual connections', this chapter will examine quite an eclectic mix. What makes a great story and what doesn't? We'll look at King Arthur and the Knights of the Round Table, the Wizard Merlin; and how film directors tried to tempt Sigmund Freud into the world of movies to use his art of storytelling.

"The pen is mightier than the sword".

Written language communication is a more effective tool than direct violence. This phrase was historically coined by English author Edward Bulwer-Lytton in 1839, but arguably it has been around historically much longer.

I've often heard it said, "Do beliefs and storytelling really have an impact?" Well let's demonstrate this with an example and take a look at historical England. Our comparatively small country, where the weather is often wet and dull, was once a powerhouse. We rose up from once living in the mud to own land based in various time zones throughout the world. So what changed us?

As one story goes, it was purported that is was the Monk of Monmouth (or Geoffrey of Monmouth) who created the legend and the mythology of King Arthur, The Knights of the Roundtable, Excalibur and Merlin. He designed magical landscapes and planted new ideas in our heads, so much so that we believed in ourselves like never before. With that confidence and conviction we rose from a life in the depths of the mud to exalted heights to influence the world.

This further illustrates the point made in Chapter 1, i.e. that stories can change beliefs and they can change how we see ourselves.

What makes a story?

Let's start to explore what makes a story, because instinctively we all know what makes a story. For example, is the following a story?

I woke up one morning and the sun was shining. I went out of my front door for a little stroll and I noticed a rabbit who said, "Good morning".
"Ahh", I thought to myself, "A talking rabbit", and I walked on home.

Instinctively you will know it's not a story but just a collection of some information. So what is it that makes a story? Let's revisit this information and see if we can turn it into a story.

I woke up one morning and the sun was shining. I went outside for a little stroll and a rabbit appeared from nowhere to bounce up to me and announce, "Help me John, there's a ferocious dog chasing me!" I looked up and sure enough a snarling dog rushed around the corner at some speed. I grabbed the rabbit as I thought to myself, "Ahh, a talking rabbit", and rushed off with the dog in chase. It nearly caught up with us as I could feel its hot breath just behind me. I quickly reached my house, got inside and hurriedly slammed the door shut before the dog could catch us.

So why is that more of a story? Well there was more substance and *something was actually happening* that was able to hold our attention. When we're telling stories to change beliefs, to set goals, to inspire or to transform, we need to remember that within the content of the story *something needs to happen.*

$100,000 for advice on movies!

There's an old saying that goes, "If it wasn't for Goliath, David would be some punk throwing a stone". Great storytellers seem to instinctively know this, but let's take a brief look behind this theory.

I'm going to turn our attention to Sigmund Freud (1856 -1939), an Austrian neurologist, founder of psychoanalysis and a great storyteller. So much so that in 1925 the head of MGM films in Hollywood, Samuel Goldwyn, offered him $100,000 to advise on movies and express psychoanalytical theory through cinema.

This is a good point to offer a little condensed Freud theory to help you grasp more meaning within the context of movies.

The id, ego, and superego are names for the three parts of the human personality which constitute Freud's psychoanalytic personality theory. All three parts are said to combine to underpin the complex behaviour of human beings. Let's consider each part:

The id is governed by the pleasure principle and tends to be the animal side of us that satisfies basic needs. For those of us who love chocolate, the moment we see it we think, "I'm going to eat that chocolate, yum, yum, yum". During prehistoric times it was not uncommon for a caveman to see somebody attractive they liked and wanted to meet. They would approach them; hit them on the head with a club to knock them out before dragging them back by the hair to the cave to declare…. "Mine now!" We're talking about instant gratification for our wants and needs and this can include safety, food and shelter.

The super ego is based on morals and judgments and the conscience to dictate the beliefs of what's right and wrong. It acts as the moral code book. Therefore when we see chocolate we may initially think, "I want some chocolate", but the moral compass says, "Oh, perhaps I could have one, possibly two bars of chocolate at the most and I'd better pay for it first". When we approach the shop counter we sometimes find ourselves buying the *two* bars of chocolate, just because the id sometimes has a tendency to win out a little.

When we see somebody attractive we may initially think to ourselves, "I must make an effort to get chatting to this person and pluck up the courage to ask them out on a date". We eventually muster the courage to go over and say, "Hi, I'm John….I noticed you sitting alone here and I wondered if I could buy you a drink and share an interesting story?" Now that's a smooth talker.

The ego is the tension that exists between the id and the super ego and is based on the reality principle. It separates out what is real and helps us to organise our thoughts and make sense of them and the world around us. The ego understands that other people have needs and desires and that sometimes being impulsive or selfish can hurt us in the long term. The ego's job is to meet the needs of the id, while taking into consideration the reality of the situation. It's a person's sense of self-esteem or self-importance.

Of course the ego is good for us, but it can generate adverse reactions from others when it gets a little too big and create a pull between the id and the upper ego.

The id creates the demands, the ego adds the needs of reality and the superego adds morality to the action taken.

How do Freud's parts apply to storytelling? Well in any story there tends to be a problem, an issue or a 'baddie' and this tends to be represented as the id. Conversely, the superego is represented by the solution or the 'goodie'.

Let's give this some meaningful context with two examples based on reasonably well-known films. I appreciate the following detail will have more meaning once you have seen the films and I would recommend them:

First example:

In the Hollywood blockbuster *Star Wars* the id is represented as Darth Vader. Once a heroic Jedi Knight he was seduced by the Dark Side of the Force, he became a Sith Lord and fought against the Empire's Jedi Order. *"Boo, hissss."*

The superego is the Jedi Knight Luke Skywalker, an important figure in the Rebel Alliance. *"Hurrah!"*

The pull between The Dark Side of the Force (the id) and the Jedi Knight (the super ego) creates the story, i.e. the ego.

If the Jedi Knights as the super ego always won out, it would make for quite a boring and predictable story. Actually, the same applies if The Dark Side always won. The tension of the pull between these two parts creates the story.

Second example:

Let's take another film, the wonderful *Shawshank Redemption*, and bear in mind that the id, super ego and ego parts do not necessarily have to be represented by people. The hero is somebody who finds himself to be an inmate at the Shawshank prison for a crime he says he didn't commit, the murder of his wife and her secret lover. It's a very clever storyline and there is no irrefutable hard evidence to support or deny the allegation throughout the movie. This continues to create some debate today and the central character, Andy Dufresne, is nonetheless represented as the superego.

So what is represented in the film as the id? Well if you consider the human face you may think it is the corrupt prison warden. However, it's actually the prison system. It's the tension that develops between the prison system (id) and the hero Andy (super ego) within this story that creates the ego and an interesting storyline.

I'm only human after all.

There seems to be something about us as humans that we love to have a moral ending and we seem to want the superego to win out. How does this apply to our stories? Well let's go back to our early morning walk in the sunshine when we met a rabbit. This was all reasonably interesting as it's rare to come across a talking rabbit. But then we added the dog and the chase. The dog represented the id and the rabbit and I became the superego. The tension between the two created a much more interesting story.

When you are looking to design a story it is worth keeping in mind Freud's parts theory to create some rich content and dynamic interaction. Who knows…..you might be invited onto the movie set as a consultant!

Where else can we apply this theory?

Managing teams of people. If you're aiming to inspire your team, and you talk exclusively about all the wonderful things they've achieved, this might sound motivational on the surface but it can also come across as a little hollow and empty. However, if you introduced some sort of obstacle, a foe or someone to pitch against, then you have something to create a collective spirit and to rally around. This creates some potential conflict and a tension which makes the objective a little more difficult to achieve. Although there is the danger of suffering a loss, it becomes possible to turn the situation around at the last minute and convert the situation into an exhilarating triumph.

Therapists/advisors helping clients. Often therapists and advisors can struggle when they attempt to provide an immediate solution to a situation, only to find that clients don't act on it? However, if the solution was designed and cleverly hidden within a story, a client can eventually discover the solution for themselves as if it was their own idea and therefore take action.

Know your audience.

Storytelling is transformational, but it's important to ensure that the story does not become too one dimensional and focus only on the positive. The addition of some obstacle or conflict will create a tension to spark real interest and intrigue to capture and hold attention.

The id is the problem or situation the client is facing. The superego represents the solution, and the tension between the two creates the interest that creates a story that holds attention, i.e. the ego. So how do we know what's going to hold the attention of the audience you are talking to? Well that's why it's important *to know and understand your audience*.

For example, you may have cleverly designed a story about football to help solve a particular problem. But if the mere mention of the word 'football' causes the person's eyes to glaze over from sheer disinterest and just switch off, they're never going to hear multiple levels of meaning in this instance. Make sure you tailor the stories and the issues in line with the interests of your audience.

Recapping the plot so far.

What have we learned in this chapter?

* How a monk took a wet little country like England and turned it into a powerhouse by talking about King Arthur, The Knights of the Roundtable and Merlin. Further evidence that stories change beliefs.

* What distinguishes basic information from a good story is the fundamental importance of ensuring that something is *happening*. The introduction of the dog in the story above added momentum and excitement to capture attention.

* That rabbits can talk a lot of sense when they need to. Was this the same rabbit turned hero from Chapter 1?

* The id, the ego, and the superego are names for the three parts of the human personality which constitute Freud's psychoanalytic personality theory. These can be applied effectively in storytelling to create tension and dynamics.

* Hollywood made some great films and The Force has been strong throughout this chapter.

* The value of introducing some conflict or obstacle to overcome within the story will hold attention.

* Stories can be used to help manage teams of people and for therapists to help clients find solutions.

* Tailor stories to meet the interests of your audience. Know your audience and make it relevant to them to captivate, engage and become meaningful.

We're now getting ready to move into Chapter 3 already. We will start to examine story structure and how this can be used if you want to write a best-selling book or movie, or indeed prepare some effective content material in readiness for a therapy session.

CHAPTER 3

THE HERO'S JOURNEY, UGLY OGRES, DONKEYS AND JEDI KNIGHTS.
- STORY STRUCTURE.

We have briefly visited the world of movies in previous chapters and discovered that they are a powerful way of reaching wide audiences and delivering key messages with storytelling. In this chapter we're going to continue to build upon this theme as we look closely at story structure.

Stories are known to build curiosity and to inspire people to act and behave in a way that can enrich their lives. Read on to hear more of a young man who set out to save a Princess from the Galactic Empire and became a hero of the Rebel Alliance to save the Galaxy. We'll also meet a talking donkey with the ability to fly, before considering whether we should take a red pill or a blue bill.

Most importantly the stories I am about to share with you are all built upon a particular *structure,* one that has ensured success and a method that you can learn to apply for yourself. Firstly I will provide some important context to explain how the structure works, before we relate this to some memorable movies.

A long time ago in a galaxy far far away.

Many of you will recognise this heading as the opening crawl of the signature device featured in every numbered film of the *Star Wars* series created by George Lucas. It's not unreasonable to say that this man was very successful. You're probably already recalling the delights of the many *Star Wars* movies and the impact their myths may have had on you and your life. However, it's not particularly well known that George Lucas was in fact guided by a mentor to achieve such acclaim. This was someone who gave him the focus needed to initially draw together the early drafts for his sprawling imaginary universe into a single storyline.

It was none other than Joseph Campbell (1904-1987) who provided the necessary blueprint that provided the structure needed to make his films a success. Campbell had some impact in 1949 in the field of mythology with his book entitled *The Hero With a Thousand Faces*, a 'must read' in Hollywood. He explored mythology from all around the world and discovered that there seemed to be a universal pattern to storytelling which he named *The Hero's Journey*.

We will tap into the universal rhythm of the storytelling to illustrate the structure of *The Hero's Journey* by considering some of the most popular and successful films. *Star Wars* (the original first movie now subtitled *Episode IV: A New Hope*) is therefore a particularly good example, but we will also extend this concept into the wonderfully animated film *Shrek (the first movie)* and the deliciously complex *The Matrix (the first in the trilogy)*. We could actually use any Hollywood movie and quote some books, but these three films have attracted the most extensive audiences and the chances are that you will be familiar with at least one of them. However, it's important to firstly be aware and understand the framework for *The Hero's Journey*.

"We can be heroes just for one day".

With his great ability to reinvent himself, David Bowie (1947-2016, English singer, songwriter and actor) was recognised to be something of a hero. One wonders what stories he would tell himself to be able to so regularly transform and achieve such well-deserved success. Known initially as an R&B singer, then Mod Rocker, to Starman, to Alien Rock Superstar Ziggy Stardust, to Thin White Duke, to Dance Rocker and concluded as an avant-garde artist. He constantly changed his story (/persona) to change his life.

Perhaps there is something you have yet to achieve, perhaps a particularly challenging ambition or interest? As I have explained above, there is a universal model that we can all tap into to design a life worth living, one that has been successfully used in the movies.

Let's now examine the framework for Joseph Campbell's *The Hero's Journey*.

The model is comprised of a number of successive stages. You will notice a pattern, or narrative that describes the typical adventure of 'The Hero', a person who uses their abilities to courageously strive to achieve great things. *Please note that there are variations to the stages that can be applied - for the purposes of allowing you to grasp a sequence that you can quickly utilise for yourself, I shall focus on the stages of the following simple model:*

(i) Hearing A Calling: A strong urge towards a particular way of life.

(ii) Accepting The Calling: The situation escalates, possibly as a result of external pressures or from something within. An acceptance to face change.

(iii) Crossing A Threshold: Likely to be a milestone or an unfamiliar change in direction. A point where The Hero has made a commitment.

(iv) Finding Your Guardians Or Mentors: Possibly seasoned travellers, often wise people met along the way that can provide support, advice or guidance for the journey.

(v) Facing A Challenge: A point of confrontation – a resistance, something becomes realised, possibly something unknown, perhaps a fear. Often referred to as trials or tests to begin transformation.

(vi) Transforming Your Demon: From the confrontation/fear something new is discovered. A new awareness is realised, a growing positivity or a new perspective emerges. The transformation of a demon into a positive resource.

(vii) Completing The Task Called For: The issue has been tackled and overcome. There is an acknowledgement, a reward or point of celebration.

(viii) Returning Home: The completion of the adventure and to bring back the reward. The conflict at the beginning has been resolved and the person is transformed to become a hero.

"Saturday night at the movies, who cares what picture you see?"

Well I'm going to narrow the choice and focus on a few of the most popular movies as explained above. However, I will also add a touch of reality to the mix to aid your understanding of the sequential stages. Together with an interpretation of the stages within those movies (*Spoiler Alert*), I will also suggest a perspective from a Therapist or Manager's viewpoint. *It's worth noting that Campbell's original model contained many more stages and I have focused on the main broad areas.*

Furthermore, you may feel there are different aspects of the films that can relate to the respective stages and that's fine. I am giving my interpretation to illustrate each of those respective stages numbered above in relation to *Star Wars*, *Shrek*, *The Matrix* and a perspective for a *Therapist or Manager*:

(i) Hearing A Calling.

Star Wars:
Luke Skywalker was living with his aunt and uncle on a moisture farm on the desert planet of Tatooine. He discovered a message stored by the droid R2-D2 that projected a hologram image of the Princess Leia that said, "Help me Obi-Wan Kanobi you're my only hope".

Shrek:
The carefree ogre Shrek lives a quiet life alone in a swamp. Unbeknown to him, Lord Farquaad exiles a number of fairy tale creatures to his swamp to ruin his way of life. Shrek seeks to find who is responsible

The Matrix:
Thomas Anderson, better known as his alias Neo, is a computer programmer/hacker who is relentlessly searching for something. Trinity is a fellow programmer/hacker who provides bait on his computer to follow the white rabbit to a club where she tells him she knows the answer to the question, "What is the Matrix?" She tells of a mysterious entity known as Morpheus and Neo receives a call from Morpheus himself on his mobile phone (quite literally 'a calling' on the mobile phone).

As a Therapist or Manager

Unlock The Power Of Stories

You may find in your day-to-day business that you are approached by a client or a member of your team for help or support, possibly in relation to a particular issue or project.

(ii) Accepting The Calling.

Star Wars:
R2-D2 leads Luke to a meeting with Obi-Wan Kenobi who provides the background to the Princess's plea. The droids and the Princess are part of an organised Rebellion against the Empire. Kenobi teaches Luke about The Force and gives him his father's light saber. Luke then leaves Tatooine to begin the quest to become a Jedi Knight.

Shrek:
The situation annoys Shrek. After questioning the fairy tale creatures he eventually discovers that Lord Farquaad is responsible and travels to his castle only to be told that he must rescue Princess Fiona in order to get his swamp back. Shrek's quest begins.

The Matrix:
Neo's time has come and he has been given that 'something' to search for – the chance to find the answer to a question that has been haunting him…'What is the Matrix?' Morpheus offers Neo a red pill (reality) or a blue pill (ignorance). The blue pill will allow him to wake up remembering nothing, but the red pill will allow Morpheus to show him where the rabbit hole leads. He's only offering the

truth and by accepting the pill Neo accepts the journey.

As a Therapist or Manager.
You will listen to the request for support from a client or team member and consider how best you might be able to help them. Of course you may want to probe to better understand the issue and gain some clarity before you make a final decision, and agree to help and accept the calling.

(iii) Crossing A Threshold.

Star Wars:
Luke's aunt and uncle are killed by storm troopers and Luke has no option but to leave Tatooine with Obi-Wan Kenobi. At the space port Mos Eisley they hire ship captain Hans Solo to take off from Tatooine. Luke crosses a threshold and leaves his past behind.

Shrek:
At the castle Shrek discovers that Lord Farquaad has set a duel to find someone to rescue Princess Fiona for him so he can marry her. He tells his knights that whoever kills Shrek will be allowed to go on the quest. Shrek defeats them and Lord Farquaad then announces that Shrek can have his swamp back only if he rescues the Princess Fiona.

The Matrix:
Neo takes and swallows the red pill. Neo enters the real world in a liquid filled pod guarded by

mechanical octopus like creatures. The threshold is crossed.

As a Therapist or Manager.
Once your client/team member has responded to your early advice and any instruction, this is a measure that they have agreed to progress to the next stage and take personal responsibility for their situation. They are prepared therefore to commit to change and move forward. As with these movies, there are likely to be a number of thresholds to be crossed as the hero moves beyond old limiting beliefs and thoughts that may have been holding them back. The very acceptance of a new idea or team project is a positive indication that the person is prepared to do something different and begin to change and transform.

(iv) Finding Your Guardians Or Mentors:
'Guardians or Mentors' wasn't the precise terminology used originally by Joseph Campbell as he used the phrases 'wise old man' and 'wise old woman'. Interestingly the guardians or mentors do not necessarily need to wise or old, and similarly they don't need to be a man or a woman.

Star Wars:
Luke is rescued by Obi-Wan Kenobi after a confrontation with the Sand People. Kenobi was then able to explain about the Jedi, The Force and Luke's father. This wise old man then offers to teach Luke the ways of the Jedi. Luke initially refuses, but as you will see above this changed when Luke discovers his home burned and family

murdered. Luke is spurred on to learn the ways of The Force and become a Jedi like his father and accepts Obi-Wan Kenobi as a mentor to guide him. We also meet the legendary Jedi master Yoda. He had a very strong connection with The Force and a major influence on Luke and so he may also regarded as a mentor.

Shrek:
This may be hard to accept, but the talking Donkey is regarded as Shrek's annoying but good hearted mentor. Despite his childlike excitement he is relatively clear minded and always looks for the positive.

The Matrix:
It is Morpheus who tests the resolve of the hero Neo to encourage him to continue with the quest - to stray from the familiar or to return to it? I did mention this was a complex movie because, ironically Neo tends to regard Morpheus as the true hero, but he was merely a supporter.

As a Therapist or Manager.
As you work so closely with your client/team member there is every chance that you will assume the role of a mentor. With the greater experience and knowledge you will take an active role to teach, guide and support based on their specific development needs.

(v) Facing A Challenge.

Star Wars:
Luke is confronted by many challenges along the way, such as his ability to master the light saber or when storm troopers attempt to stop him leaving Tatooine. But perhaps the most significant was Darth Vader, a Jedi Knight himself, but one who was seduced by the Dark Side of The Force to serve the evil Galactic Empire.

Shrek:
There are a number of physical challenges such as rescuing Donkey from the Lava Lake and from The Dragon, fighting robbers and kidnappers and then removing his helmet to let the Princess see what he really looked like. Then we see the challenge of an emotional relationship between Shrek and Princess Fiona. Shrek falls in love with Princess Fiona but is very much afraid of his own feelings as he pondered, "How would it be possible for her to love an ogre?"

The Matrix:
Neo learns about the Matrix and his capability with it, the dangers of Agents, how to fight and who his friends are. However, the main challenge is arguably when Neo faces his demons, Agent Smith and the falling green Matrix Code.

As a Therapist or Manager.
This is where the problem or issue has now been identified for the client/team member. They now need to confront and tackle the key thing that is

perceived as an obstacle. Quite often we find this doesn't run smooth and there is much learning to be had along the way. Team support can be valuable as a group stands united in combatting a difficult challenge head on and together.
There may well be ups and downs along the way, but *oh the places you'll go!*

(vi) Transforming Your Demon.

Star Wars:
Luke also starts to realise that he is a significant factor in ensuring that the rebels succeed and that he could play a significant part in the fall of The Empire. There is reconciliation between Luke and Darth Vader and Luke attempts to save Vader who transpires to be his own father.

Shrek:
Shrek and Donkey travel to Farquaad's castle to deliver Princess Fiona. The journey is broken to rest for the night and Donkey discovers that the Princess also transforms into an ogre after sunset. Shrek overhears a conversation Princess Fiona has with Donkey when she explains her concern that no one could love a hideous beast. She was referring *to her own transformed appearance*, but Shrek mistakenly thinks she was referring to him and becomes disheartened. Aware of Shrek's feelings for the Princess, it was Donkey's later intervention that helped him transform *the demon* and to think otherwise by talking him into declaring his love for her. But time is pressing and Shrek realises it may

now be too late to stop her wedding with Lord Farquaad.

The Matrix:
At last Neo begins to believe in his abilities and turns his fear into focus. But the agents track him down and Agent Smith shoots him dead in a hallway. Trinity confesses her love for him to his unconscious body and Neo experiences a resurrection. He wakes up to start to see the green computer coding around him and effectively use his abilities to stop bullets mid-air before finishing off Agent Smith.

As a Therapist or Manager.
The problems and challenges that face your client/team member can represent an opportunity to turn their lives around. The positive influence of the mentor can instil a sense of purpose, achievement and a growing confidence along the way. There comes a point when there may be a realisation that it is truly possible to overcome and tackle the problem.

Let's not forget Malcolm Gladwell's book *David and Goliath*; a story of an underdog who successfully outsmarted the strong. By overcoming perceptions of size that seemed to hold him back, David was able to turn that demonic thought into the positive resources of speed and agility to defeat his foe.

For one who is dyslexic, I have faced a similar battle to confront and overcome my demons and turn my life around. Having transformed the threat into an opportunity I am now running a successful business as a Master Trainer and NLP Master Practitioner. I now share my learning and knowledge with others to help transform their lives.

NB: Neuro Linguistic Programming (NLP) is a method of influencing the brain as a result of the language and varied communication patterns we use. It's how these interact and run together, much like a computer program, to manifest new behaviour to affect us as individuals.

(vii) Completing The Task Called For:

Star Wars:
The Death Star is destroyed and Luke saves the galaxy from the Dark Side. He now trusts The Force and joins the rebel fleet as a pilot. He is then able to venture into a galaxy that's no longer so far far away.

Shrek:
Shrek runs into the church to stop the wedding and publicly declares his love for the Princess. Mayhem follows but Donkey arrives riding The Dragon who devours and kills Lord Farquaad. Shrek recovers his swampland, marries Princess Fiona and has the ability to make new friends.

The Matrix:
Neo is now able to manipulate the green Matrix coding and begins to control it.

As a Therapist or Manager.

The issue or problem has been successfully addressed and it's now possible to see the change in your client/team member and how a transformation has taken place.

(viii) Returning Home.

Star Wars:
The return home is not necessarily so literal. For many, it is the recognition that Princess Leia is Luke's sister and that the two come together as family. Now it becomes clear why any attempt by Luke at a romantic link was unsuccessful and why the Princess was drawn to Hans Solo.
(For Star Wars aficionados this revelation surfaces during the Return of the Jedi. The return home is being awarded by the alliance, and becoming part of the alliance "family".)

Shrek:
This is a physical return home for Shrek as he goes back to the Swamp.

The Matrix:
Neo returns home to Zion, the last human city on the planet Earth, to show an acceptance that he is truly 'The One'. He brings a hope for ending the war with the Machines and unplugging the rest of the helpless humans from the Matrix. He becomes a saviour for mankind.

As a Therapist or Manager.
Joseph Campbell's *The Hero's Journey* stresses the importance of supporting others on their journey.
Once your clients and team colleagues have fully grown and transformed as a result of their journey, they then have the opportunity to strive to support others on their journey by passing on their new found knowledge and learning experiences.

Some of these movies have had prequels and sequels.
- The *Star Wars* prequels featured a young Obi-Wan Kenobi and Yoda when they first began to build their learning and experiences to later share with Luke.
- *Shrek 2* is a continuation of the original film when it's time to meet the parents and there's some tension. In many ways Shrek becomes the mentor of the disapproving King who undertakes a similar journey of self-discovery to Shrek.
- There are some mixed viewed about the remaining films in the *Matrix* trilogy and the issue of passing on the learning is less clear, however, you may have your own view.

When you next watch a movie, in particular a Hollywood movie, be aware of the stages given above and you'll find that you can just tick them of as you move from scene to scene and the story unfolds.

Recapping the plot so far.

What have we learned in this chapter?

* Stories are known to build curiosity and to inspire people to act and behave in a way that can enrich their lives.

* Your beliefs are based on the stories you tell yourself and others. Change your story and change your life.

* A particular framework has been used for many years in the movies for successful story telling. Joseph Campbell provided the blueprint that became a universal model we can all tap into to design a life worth living. This has given movie writers the focus to produce a real Blockbuster.

* The model is comprised of a number of successive stages creating a pattern, or narrative, that describes the typical adventure of 'The Hero'

* You can identify characters in many movies that can be used to fit Joseph Campbell's blueprint for storytelling.

* You have much in common with Luke Skywalker, Shrek and Neo in that as soon as you hear and accept the calling, you can begin a wonderful journey of your own to overcome your fears and make a real success of your life. There are also many inspirational female heroes in the movies

where this framework could also apply; Katniss Everdeen (The Hunger Games), Ellen Ripley (Alien) and Clarice Starling (Silence of the Lambs) to name but a few.

* Once the journey is completed, it's important to share the knowledge and learning with others to help them along their journey.

* It's almost impossible to complete a full chapter without making references to *rabbits*. Did you spot them?

The Hero's Journey is just one of a number of different storytelling structures. As we move into the next chapter you will learn of yet more effective frameworks that will allow you to help change and transform not only your own life, but the lives of others.

CHAPTER 4

MIRROR NEURONS, MONKEYS, ISOMORPHIC METAPHORS, PIXAR AND FISH.
- MORE STORY FRAMEWORKS.

The journey into the world of storytelling frameworks will draw to an end in the coming chapters. Not to worry though, because you will have the reward of much learning to take with you as you embark on new stories of your own. You will turn the last page with the opportunity to change and become a real hero yourself.

This may sound somewhat extreme, but now that you better understand the power of structured storytelling you can reflect on all the great achievements in your life and how they came about. They are likely to have been as a result of the stories you told yourself.

We'll continue to stick with a winning formula and tempt you with a mixture of seemingly disparate subjects that can be combined to concoct a recipe for success. You're probably already wondering, "What on earth are Mirror Neurons and Isomorphic Metaphors?" and, "How could they possibly relate to monkeys, the American film studio Pixar and fish?"

Let's reflect on neurons.

Dr. Giacomo Rizzolatti is a neurophysiologist of the University of Parma, Italy. Born in Kiev, Ukraine in 1937 he had a long standing interest in how the brain connects to movement. As a result of studies undertaken with the macaque monkey, he discovered a unique type of neuron called 'Mirror Neurons' and found techniques that would demonstrate this in humans.

Let's briefly step back to explain that *neurons* are cells within the nervous system that transmit information to other nerve cells, muscle, or gland cells. A *mirror neuron* is a neuron that fires both when we act *and* when we observe the same action performed by another. So in effect it 'mirrors' the behaviour of another as though you were acting yourself, i.e. a person takes action as well as when he or she perceives it.

Put simply, mirror neurons help us to learn and a classic example is when you watch children who mimic adults. You may remember a television advertisement produced by the UK Government that showed how children would so easily copy their parents when smoking. They could be seen using pens, pencils or anything as a substitute for cigarettes. It's true; children will do what an adult does, but not necessarily what they say. This is perhaps a simplistic way of explaining that mirror neurons allow us to mimic the behaviour of people around us and learn very quickly. Therefore, you can see how this concept can be used to our advantage by observing excellent skills in others that will allow you to emulate yourself as the mirror neurons fire in your brain.

The work of Dr. Giacomo Rizzolatti is powerful and it's no wonder he has achieved *Rock Star status* in the world of neuroscience. However, can you imagine that there is in fact another way to fire mirror neurons to achieve the same result? Well, this can be done by telling stories.

Storytelling will fire mirror neurons in the brain so that it trains a person to behave and act in the way described in the story. You can now begin to see the potential this concept holds and to understand when people remark that storytelling is the key to influencing and transforming people to achieve change. You may also begin to appreciate that some of the very best teachers, trainers and leaders use stories to illustrate their points to encourage learning. Think back to any non-fiction book you have read, training course attended or keynote speech delivered and take a minute to remember the stories that illustrated the points being made. Aren't these the parts of the book or course that you more easily remember - perhaps they even repeat or affect your beliefs and approach now?

"The needs of the many outweigh the needs of the one" (see Appendix **).

Such a statement created quite an emotional scene between Spock and Captain Kirk in the *Star Trek* film, *The Wrath of Khan* (1982). It's an interesting point and the flip side to, "The needs of the one outweigh the needs of the many". Both statements feature in the film at different points, and again in *The Search for Spock* (1984), but before we get drawn into yet another intriguing story, the point is that there are different perspectives to consider depending upon the circumstances at the time.

We have indicated that we would explore some different storytelling structures throughout this book. In the previous chapter we explored *The Hero's Journey*, a classic well known story structure often used in movies and presented to the widest of audiences around the world. Such films carry a generic message and are likely to have a random impact upon individuals by stirring their thinking to positively behave and act in a different way.

However, the ability to design and create a more unique story tailored directly to meet the needs of a particular person, the one, or even a group, is likely to be even more powerful and effective. But is there possibly a structure that exists to help us individually live long and prosper? Well yes there is, read on.

Isomorphic metaphor.

We're now going to explore a particular story structure taken from the world of Neuro Linguistic Programming (NLP).

NLP has a range of very powerful techniques and we are going to focus on something called the *Isomorphic Metaphor*. This looks to be quite a daunting term but it is just a label. From typical dictionary definitions, you'll know that a *metaphor* describes a person or object by referring to something that is considered to have similar characteristics to that person or object, e.g. 'the city is a jungle' or 'life is a roller coaster' etc. The prefix of *Isomorphic* simply means 'corresponding' or 'similar' in form and relations between two groups, i.e. they share the same structure. So it becomes possible to construct a metaphorical story that has the same key elements, events and subjects based on a real life situation.

This now raises the question, "How do you design an isomorphic metaphor?" and we're going to take a look at the example David Gordon gave in his book *Therapeutic Metaphors*. He used the metaphor as a tool for changing behaviours through therapy. He would collect a wealth of important information about a client and effectively use this to outline the particular challenges they faced, together with a possible solution, through the design of a parallel metaphorical story. His book explains a particular framework to achieve this. Let's take a look.

The design process or framework.

(i) The actual situation. Significant persons and the problem.

There is a process we can use to help design the isomorphic metaphor for any given situation. Simply take a sheet of paper and fold it in half to create two columns. Down the left hand side begin to list all the significant persons involved and how the problem develops or progresses within the actual situation. We therefore list the component parts of 'Father', 'Mother' and 'Son' down the left hand column to reflect all members of the 'Family'. We also add the word 'Family'.
(Don't worry this is all clarified below, but for now please follow this example – it's a scenario proposed by David Gordon that features the members of a family).

Now in addition to listing the people involved we now continue by providing some information about the situation that was challenging this family and what was actually happening, i.e. the progression of the problem. Well the father was rarely home - so we now add 'Father rarely home'. As a consequence of this, and the absence of the head of household, the son tends to get into trouble - so we add 'Son gets into trouble'. In these circumstances the mother would cover for the son and when the father finds out he becomes furious and leaves. Without a solution this situation becomes self-perpetuating and would just recycle endlessly. So we add 'Mother covers for son', 'Father finds out, becomes furious and leaves' and 'No resolution, problem recycles'.

The left hand column lists all the significant people involved together with the events that are happening as the problems progress. We are now ready to design a story to change that behaviour and achieve a different outcome. We have stressed in Chapter 2 the importance of knowing your audience to make the story meaningful. From the information known about this family, it was clear that they had a keen interest in sailing. He designed the story around the theme of 'sailing' with a view to changing the current behaviour and transforming this family. But how did he do that?

(ii) The metaphor. Story characters and story structure.

David Gordon created a structure based on some clever metaphorical references for the family members based on the situation. He focused on the right hand column of the folded paper to feature the metaphorical story characters and story structure, i.e. *'isomorphism'* is the metaphorical preservation of the relationship occurring in the actual problem situation.

Directly in line with each item he listed a suitable representative metaphor associated with 'sailing'. Therefore in the right hand column, adjacent to 'Father', he wrote the story character of the Ship's 'Captain', 'Mother' became '1st Mate' and 'Son' became 'Cabin boy'. Hopefully you can see how these parallel distinctions are shaping up and so adjacent to 'Family' he wrote 'Boat Crew'. This concludes the representations for the significant people involved, so let's move on to the progression of the problem with the behaviours being displayed.

Next on the list was 'Father rarely home'. So how can we characterise this without removing the 'Captain' from the boat? Well this can be represented by 'Captain often shut up in cabin'. Next on the left-hand list is 'Son gets into trouble' and so this behaviour transfers to 'Cabin boy sets the wrong sails'. Hopefully you're now following the flow and can anticipate that 'Mother' as '1st Mate' covers for the 'Cabin boy' by correcting him and trying to reset the sails before the 'Captain' sees. From the original situation we know that 'Father finds out, becomes furious and leaves' and so in the story this becomes 'Captain finds out, furious he was not told and retires to his cabin'.

Similar to the actual story, the metaphorical story continues without a resolution and so the concluding point in the right hand column is 'No resolution, problem recycles *until*....'

(iii) Finding a resolution.

There is no resolution to the problem and so the situation just continues until a solution can be found to break the cycle. This layout provides a simple structure and flow to the story to make it possible to add the detail to the metaphorical story and provide a conclusion that can relate back to the actual situation. For reasons that will become clear as you continue to read, I am not focusing too heavily on the resolution in Gordon's story. Nonetheless, in his example the solution was found when the '1st Mate' reminded the 'Captain' of his own behaviour when he was a youth. This then influenced how the 'Captain' responded to the 'Cabin boy' and a similar approach can then be applied to the 'Father' and 'Son' back in the actual situation. The resolution was elaborately woven into the fabric of the story to improve impact.

For those who have trained in Neuro Linguistic Programming (NLP) it is possible to significantly enhance the metaphorical story and achieve the most amazing results by embedding and hiding NLP language patterns (as determined by the great Milton Erickson, an American psychologist who specialised in medical hypnosis and family therapy. 1901-1980). These patterns are known to *generalise, distort and delete* information which allows the person's unconscious mind to fill in any blanks and make a unique interpretation.

Once you have carefully written and told your metaphorical story using the characters and story structure, it's fair to assume that *you* will have provided a particular solution. However, no matter how clever you think that solution might be, it is for that person to find their own interpretation and one that is just right for them. *This is why it is so important to resist the urge to explain how you composed your story and to allow their unconscious mind to create a meaning that works for them.*

You may now begin to see how wonderfully simple and elegant this approach to storytelling can be at achieving real transformation and helping people change. In NLP terms, what we are essentially doing is *pacing* somebody else's world and then *leading* them into a new way of thinking by keeping the verbs and action words, but changing the names.

To clarify.

The following is an overview of the set of transformations as adapted from David Gordon's book. For each character or issue, we are going to consider the **'Actual Situation'** and how this translates to a corresponding **'Metaphor'** in the story.

Firstly, we'll examine each **'Significant Person'** and convert them to a 'Story Character'.

Father = Captain.
Mother = 1st Mate.
Son = Cabin Boy.
Family = Boat Crew.

Secondly, we'll then consider the **'Progression of the Problem'** and convert these to the '**Story Structure'**.

Father rarely home = Captain often shut up in cabin.

Son gets into trouble = Cabin boy sets the wrong sails.
Mother covers for son = 1st Mate corrects him and tries to reset sails before Captain sees.
Father finds out, becomes furious and leaves = Captain finds out, furious he was not told and retires to cabin.
No resolution, problem recycles = No resolution, problem recycles until……..

Thirdly, we need to consider the '**Solution**' for the actual situation and relate this to the '**Solution**' in the metaphorical story.

The solution is influenced by the metaphorical outcome. In this example the '1st Mate' (Mother) reminded the 'Captain' (Father) of his own impulsive behaviour when he was young. Therefore, relating this back to the actual situation helps to improve the Father's understanding. He then becomes more accepting and forgiving of the situation, loses the anger and the problem becomes resolved.

The Pixar Framework.

We're now moving onto another storytelling framework and this one is taken from a book by the Daniel Pink. Born in America in 1964 he is one of the world's leading business thinkers and the author of a number of best-selling books about work, management, and behavioral science. We're going to turn our attention to *To Sell Is Human, The Surprising Truth About Persuading, Convincing, and Influencing Others.* This explores the power of selling in our lives.

In this book Pink talks about how to become better at sales and in particular how to become better at personal selling. To become equipped to excel in the future he suggests the importance of learning particular skills, including the ability to pitch. He explains the value of explaining your ideas quickly, succinctly and persuasively. He suggests a number of ways of doing this, but there is one in particular which is appealing and memorable. He then makes a link with storytelling and indicates how stories can be very persuasive, but sometimes difficult to make them concise enough to be useable. Pink explains how stories used by Pixar (now owned by Disney) for its movies follow a particular format, one that encourages conciseness and discipline.

Back in 2012 the Pixar Story Artist, Emma Coats, revealed 22 storytelling tips on social media (Twitter). The list circulated the internet for many months and gained the popular title 'Pixar's 22 Rules of Storytelling'. Rule number 4 had particular interest and starts with 'Once upon a time'; it has become known as 'The Story Spine'. Speculation followed that this did not originate with Pixar, but instead with the writer/director/teacher Brian McDonald. He has since gone on record to explain that it wasn't his either, but he had used the format in his books, classes and lectures. He even investigated himself to try and ascertain the origins, but without success. This is quite a story in itself.

Emma Coats explained how Pixar used 'The Story Spine' framework and how it runs central to each movie narrative. The Pixar movies appear to all follow a six-sentence format to create a simple and effective storytelling template. These six phrases were used to start a sentence and to encourage a flow for the outline of the story:

Once upon a time
_____

Every day
_____

One day
_____

Because of that,
_____

Because of that, *(repeated)*
_____

Until finally
_____

Let's apply this to the well-known Pixar film *Finding Nemo* to see how it aligns with the plot:

Once upon a time, *there was a widowed fish, named Marlin, who was extremely protective of his only son, Nemo.* **Every day**, *Marlin warned Nemo of the ocean's dangers and implored him not to swim far away.* **Then one day**, *in an act of defiance, Nemo ignores his father's warnings and swims into the open water.* **Because of that**, *he is captured by a diver and ends up in the fish tank of a dentist in Sydney.* **Because of that**, *Marlin sets* *off on a journey to recover Nemo, enlisting the help of other sea creatures along the way.* **Until finally,** *Marlin and Nemo find each other, reunite, and learn that love depends on trust.*

Yes, that truly sums up the movie *Finding Nemo*.

Even the historic UK Prime Minister, Winston Churchill, once said, "All the great things are simple". You can see how this simple framework is a way of creating great structure very quickly to allow you to tell stories to other people.

It's worth noting that Brian McDonald has also mentioned that a step was omitted from the original story spine tweet: 'And ever since that day'. He believes that the list keeps getting copied with the missing step and it's an important step. This step can indicate a permanent/sustained change following the initial achievement, i.e. embedding the learning and maintaining the new state.

Oh how we love stories and I could rabbit on for ages, but for now just prick up your ears as we hop over to review this chapter.

Recapping the plot so far.

What have we learned in this chapter?

* It was Dr. Giacomo Rizzolatti's studies with monkeys that revealed the fascinating relationship between the brain and movement. That *mirror* *neurons* fire both when we act and when we observe the same action performed by others.

* Mirror neurons help us to learn and these can be triggered just as effectively through storytelling. The very best teachers, trainers and leaders use stories to illustrate their points to encourage learning.

* Generic story structures will appeal to wide audiences, but it's possible to tailor a story to suit the needs of an individual using *isomorphic metaphors*. David Gordon's framework is very effective in converting actual situations into metaphorical stories to help find resolution.

* The combination of Neuro Linguistic Programming (NLP) language patterns with storytelling has the ability to create the most profoundly positive outcomes.

* Although you think you may have cleverly created a wonderful resolution to the problem within the isomorphic metaphor, it's important not to explain how you composed your story. *Allow the person to determine their own interpretation and what's right for them.*

* The Story Spine template that fundamentally uses six sentences is a very effective, yet simple framework for structuring a story.

* We nearly got through a whole chapter without mentioning 'rabbit' once, or did we? Is the 'rabbit' a

golden thread in this book I wonder? If so, how could it possibly be linked to *change*?

"Would you tell me, please, which way I ought to go from here?"
"That depends a good deal on where you want to get to."
"I don't much care where –"
"Then it doesn't matter which way you go."
- Lewis Carroll, Alice in Wonderland

So where shall we go from here?

"Begin at the beginning," the King said, very gravely, "and go on till you come to the end: then stop."
- Lewis Carroll, Alice in Wonderland

CHAPTER 5

STORYTELLING ....BUT WHERE TO START?
- START AT THE BEGINNING.

Now that we've looked at some of the theories and models behind storytelling, let's roll up our sleeves, get our hands dirty and start to write some stories.

Having read this far, you are likely to have determined that this book is not primarily about writing novels or fiction. The key goal is to be able to effectively use the art of storytelling with your work and personal life. Stories are designed to have impact, influence and transformation in our own lives and for others. As you build your storytelling skills you will develop the potential to become a great leader in your respective field. Do respect this powerful skill we're about to hone; take responsibility and use it for the greater good (see Appendix *).

The question becomes, "Where do you start to develop stories?" Personally, I realised storytelling was a key skill but I never quite knew where to start, consequently I tended to flounder and struggled to write anything meaningful that would have impact. To avoid this happening to you, and to help you get off to a flying start, we will cover in this chapter:

* Areas in work and life where you can use storytelling

* Stories that influence

* The precursors to storytelling

* What stories to develop first and why?

* Your personal story and philosophy in life

* A step-by-step process for developing the story

* Memorable stories that 'stick' with us

* The ability to create a catalogue of stories; a resource that can be referred to for different purposes

* Taking a look at different types of stories that we may want in different areas of our lives and which models would be most applicable

The excitement of starting to write something influential and meaningful can be quite exhilarating ……so let's start.

In what areas can storytelling be used effectively?

There are many and you are limited by your own imagination, so let's consider some. The following isn't exhaustive, but you'll gain a sense of possibility:

In Business.

A key area is likely to be within a business context. This could be entrepreneurship (setting up a business, taking on financial risks in the hope of profit), or leadership (managing people and teams within a company or organisation). Stories could then be effectively used to:

* Introduce yourself to your colleagues or perhaps explain a form of branding

* Gain and exert authority. To instruct, make decisions and enforce obedience – to maintain power and control, i.e. why you should be listened to

* Reduce the time it takes to establish leadership and, at the same time, convey empathy, i.e. as human beings we are alike and we share morals, principles and goals. Involve staff in the decision making processes and let them to take some responsibility for the organisation. Encourage them to become ambassadors to speak positively and defend reputation, i.e. create Employee Engagement

* Create and sustain bonds amongst teams and colleagues to demonstrate unity when facing opposition. At the same time create trust and believability

* Present company philosophy and foster the ability to challenge other people's philosophies

* Install values and beliefs with team members and link them with the purpose and goals of the organisation. Gain and build credibility to bring people with you to achieve a common cause

* Build confidence, engage and inspire employees to produce world class levels of innovation, productivity and performance

In Teaching.

For children and students of every age:

* Stories to bring information and facts alive. To captivate, enthral and inspire by making the information 'sticky' so that it stays with them

* Humanising and making information relevant to everyday life

* Offer insights into universal life experiences

* Experience and embrace diverse cultures and celebrate differences

* Increase willingness to communicate thoughts and feelings

* Encourage imagination and creativity

* Encourage participation and enhance listening skills

In Therapy.

Storytelling in therapy is often regarded as a component of the assessment and intervention process. Stories can be cleverly used to help identify characters and issues. These often lead to increased self-disclosure, especially for those who have difficulty expressing themselves verbally. Stories have been known to help:

* Deliver an indirect form of therapy when somebody is particularly stuck and unable to move forward with their issues

* Install new beliefs and values and open up new ways of thinking

* Install coping strategies and begin the healing journey

You may see some commonality amongst these particular specialisms. Indeed, stories teach lessons, share messages and motivate. In all the above examples, stories deliver an underlying concept of influence or transformation to achieve change at some level.

Stories to influence.

The word '*influence*' is very powerful and it's worth exploring it carefully to understand precisely what it means. According to the Cambridge dictionary, 'influence' means "To affect all change, how someone or something develops, behaves or thinks". I like to dig a little deeper and conduct a simple *linguistic analysis* - a comparatively simple process that requires you to do no more than delve and probe a little deeper into the dictionary. So rather than settle with the initial definition, I look up any subsequent related words given which I may not fully understand in this context. By continuously looking up words I am able to form a broader definition to improve understanding.

Therefore, I have chosen to explore some key words within the above definition of *'influence'* – these are *'affect'*, *'change'*, *'develop'*, *'behave'* and *'think'*.

'Affect' means, "To have an influence on someone or something or to cause a change in someone or something". I'm happy with that explanation and ready to move onto the next word.

'Change' means, "To exchange one thing for another thing, especially of a similar type". I now feel the need to further explore *'exchange'* and *'especially'* to better understand the context with *'influence'*. *'Exchange'* is defined as, "To give something to someone and receive something from that person". *'Especially'* is given as, "Very much, more than usual or more than other people or things".

Now remember that all this detail is to be considered within the context of the word *'influence'* and a clearer picture is now beginning to emerge that is very positive. Combining the elements I have discovered reads something like: 'To give something to someone, to receive something, to give more than usual'. This is causing me to reconsider and change my understanding of what we mean by the word *'influence'*.

'Develop'. I'm quite happy with this so far and am ready to move on to **'Develop'**. This is defined as, "To cause something to grow or change into a more advanced, larger or stronger form". I find this interesting and now want to explore the words *'grow'*, *'advanced'*, *'larger'* and *'stronger'* - all within the context of *'influence'*.
'Grow': "To increase in size or amount, or to become more advanced or developed."
'Advanced': "More difficult level."
'Larger': "Big in size or amount."
'Stronger': "Skilled or good at doing something, powerful."

I'm now able to consider these definitions more holistically. It now suggests to me that part of *'influence'* is to 'help someone advance and develop to a more difficult level in a skilled and powerful way'. My understanding is growing even more, so let's check out those last few words to complete the picture.

'Behave': "To act in a particular way." My insight here is that *'influence'* is not just a random behaviour or language. It is quite particular or specific and, by its design, it sounds very much to me like a structured story.

'Think': "To believe something or have an opinion or idea." This definition has prompted me to look up *'believe'*, *'opinion'* and *'idea'*.
'Believe': "To think that something is true."
'Opinion': "A thought or belief about something or someone."
'Idea': "Suggestion or plan for doing something."

Hopefully you can now see that this process has unearthed much more positive detail about the word *'influence'*. To conclude the linguistic analysis it is worth checking out words or phrases that have the same or nearly the same meaning as *'influence'*. Such synonyms include: *'lead'*, *'act'*, *'inspiration'*, *'guide'* and *'force'*. The connotations for *'force'* may appear to be somewhat aggressive and perhaps negative, but I believe it is a reflection of strength or power.

We now have a thorough understanding of what *'influence'* means and what are we trying to achieve when influencing somebody with storytelling. It spans the following:

Attraction
Connection
Acceptance of our position, or what we're advocating
Sales or purchases
Involvement
Loyalty
Retention
Knowledge

Different behaviour
Transformation
Healing
Saving somebody's life
An engaged team
Motivation

The precursors to storytelling

When telling a story, how can you be sure it will have the desired effect? A simple but fundamental question, because it doesn't matter how cleverly the story has been designed, you can never be sure that someone is going to listen. If this happens then it won't be possible to establish any connection with the audience and this will lead to an inability to influence and create any transformation. So how do we engage the listener in order to succeed?

There appears to be four fundamental keys to engage the listener in the type of stories that will move them in a particular direction. These keys to influence are extremely powerful and rarely spoken about in the context of storytelling. To influence and create impact, the listener must be *fascinated* with the way you have structured and ordered the content of the story. They must feel they share common *values* with you. They must also *believe* you care about them and be able to derive some value from any perceived *relationship* they expect to have with you.

Master the skills of *fascination, values, belief and relationships* with your storytelling and you will be in a position to create the greatest opportunities through influence. You will need to exercise some caution with this as storytelling can create the potential to generate a cult-like following and the suggestion that you have some kind of authority or power over others. Remember, "With great power comes great responsibility" (see Appendix *).

In her book entitled *The Story Factor*, Annette Simmons (keynote speaker and expert storyteller) said, "Once people make your story their story, you have tapped into the powerful force of faith. Future influence will require little follow-up energy from you and may even expand as people recall and retell your story to others".

What is the principle that underlies fascination? "Fascination is one step beyond interest. Interested people want to know if it works. Fascinated people want to learn how it works." Jim Rohn (American entrepreneur, author and motivational speaker. 1930 – 2009).

What is the difference between interest and fascination? Interested people want to know what somebody is doing, where they're going and how they live. This interest often forms the basis of many TV shows such as *The Lifestyles of The Rich and Famous* and *The Kardashians*. However, fascinated people want to know the story behind the story, i.e. Why and how did they do it? What makes this person tick? Where did they come from? This clearly implies that you don't really influence others if you're just interesting. Influence comes from being fascinating.

The great Jim Rohn also said, "Learn how to turn frustration into fascination. You will learn more being fascinated by life than you will by being frustrated by it". This can have value for both you personally and when telling a story to another person.

If you are personally faced with a situation that isn't quite going your way it's easy to become frustrated, which can lead to inaction/procrastination. However, if you can become interested by both the positive and negative aspects and start to enquire and investigate the circumstances, you will gradually build a fascination. This will allow you to learn more and begin to understand what has actually happened and in turn create a mindset to find a resolution. This may not happen every time and certainly takes some practice, but it's a skill worth mastering.

Now that you have understood this, it becomes a little easier to understand and apply this when telling a story to another person. When designing the story content it's important to elicit and have their frustrations in mind. You will then be able to weave a tale of success in that particular area and how it is possible to draw upon resources to manage and overcome problems to achieve success. The story can be generic and not specifically targeted at the individual, nonetheless, the individual will make associations as the narrative becomes fascinating and they'll think, "How did he do that?" This fascination can create an image in the mind of the solution you want to influence somebody to take and a desired outcome can then become more plausible, realistic and achievable. If you see a smile creeping across their face, you'll know that you have been fascinating and that you are having some impact.

What stories to develop first and why?

I want to suggest that the first story to start to work on and develop is your own personal story. This will bring into play the keys to influence outlined above and engage the listener: *fascination, values, belief and relationships.*

It may not seem to be particularly obvious, but there will be many instances when you will be required to introduce yourself and convey an immediate impression. This will be important for networking, making connections, building rapport quickly, selling an idea, service or product. As a leader or manager it would also allow you to foster sound employee engagement.

Of course this implies that you do have a range of different stories you can draw upon that can be adapted and designed to connect with other people in different ways. You may scratch your head at this point and think that you don't have any such stories – but if you reflect on life experiences and how you have overcome issues in the past, they will come to mind. Of course what you share with people is up to you, but disclosure about yourself can demonstrate human vulnerability that can be endearing. This may cause people to care about you without undermining your authority as an individual, a leader, a manager or an entrepreneur. For many it is a bold step, but it is an opportunity to publicly share your values and beliefs and allow your audience to strike up an affinity and an empathy with you and what you represent.

Still scratching your head? Well let's consider a few varied examples:

(i) I will lead by example and you would have already read about the difficulties I faced since the age of seven with my parents, hardship and being diagnosed with dyslexia. It's is only in recent years as a Master Trainer that I decided to share this with students on my training courses. I remember struggling to record an exercise on a flipchart in class when certain words didn't seem to look right. I had a feeling that the letters of the words were all there, but not necessarily in the right order. For some strange reason I found myself saying, "Dyslexia is a difficult enough word to say, let alone spell", and so my secret was out. From that moment the attitude and interaction with my students changed. They became aware of the extreme efforts I would make for their benefit to instil learning and ensure they progressed in life. Invariably they all responded in kind. They would then go out of their way to participate, support, encourage and motivate me to drive them forward.

They showed great empathy and we discovered common values and beliefs that have led to the most enduring relationships. Many students have realised what it can take to succeed and I often wonder why I did not share this sooner.

(ii) Reality TV shows, you either love them or hate them, but they seem to follow a consistently successful formula. If you place a group of high profile celebrities/people in a harsh environment to face challenges, not only do the shifting group dynamics become apparent, but you are likely to quickly become aware of their vulnerability and their personal stories as they unfold. Whether they have become ensconced on a desert island, huddled together in a jungle or paired in a dance studio, the public will observe and engage. As personal stories emerge, viewers will look for a leader/survivor/winner with common values and beliefs to emerge successful. Quite often these celebrities/people have subsequently gone on to enjoy a renewed lease on life and career as they have also learnt more about themselves and their potential. There have been revelations because personal information contained within their stories has been divulged. They have also been known to subsequently say, "I wish I'd done it sooner".

(iii) Althea was a successful manager in a large corporate organisation. She had been consistently achieving targets and maintaining high performance standards. But in times of austerity, the organisation became faced with inevitable cuts and the need to reduce resources and achieve efficiency savings. This may sound familiar, but it falls to the leader to manage the situation as best they can and this can often mean making painful decisions on redundancy and so it carries a heavy responsibility. Her team was devastated by events. Prolonged and repeated reduction exercises took their toll on the manager as her health began to suffer until depression was diagnosed. This adversely impacted on her ability to manage and make meaningful decisions.

She chose to keep her health a secret and the situation mounted until it reached a critical tipping point as serious errors began to arise. She was called to report to her senior managers for an explanation and in tears divulged her story. This was a turning point. The managers had no idea and immediately intervened to provide help and support. Before going on a period of sick leave to recover, she also met with her team to provide a full explanation for her recent behaviour and the constraints placed on the organisation. The team had previously shared common values and beliefs in achieving their goals and were immediately empathetic and supportive. The manager returned to a more stable organisation and team in six months' time to effectively resume duties, and subsequently collect a professional award for a pioneering project in her business sector. With regard to disclosure and sharing such personal information, what did she say? "I wish I had done it sooner".

Hopefully examples will now start to come to mind and you will be able to develop your own catalogue of stories to draw upon from when needed for specific situations.

Developing your personal story

So where do we start if we want to develop storytelling that will fascinate and influence people for the good? I believe the place to start is with your personal story and this is because it demonstrates your first steps in becoming successful and building a level of authority. Your authority can be effectively derived from your story better than any resumé, qualification or any other credentials.

Here are some examples of some popular authoritative figures and the stories they represent:

- Robin Hood: hero of the people
- Oprah Winfrey: wisdom
- Tony Robbins: personal power
- Martha Stewart: class
- Jack Welch: tough-minded leadership
- Steve Jobs: innovation and creativity

Is this important? Yes, because this means you have the opportunity to reinvent yourself with a new story. Let's take the example of Al Gore, former Vice President of the United States. During his earlier career he was rebuffed by the Clintons, but subsequently he became a successful entrepreneur and someone capable of saving the world. He achieved what scientists failed to do for years and proved the threat of global warming to win a Nobel Prize. He went on to become a successful businessman, author and public speaker.

Suze Orman (Susan Lynn) was born in 1951 in Chicago and suffered a speech impediment during her early years. Her father Morry worked in a chicken factory while her mother worked as a secretary for a local rabbi. Her family constantly struggled with financial issues while she was growing up. Morry's business burnt down when Suze was just 14 years old. His subsequent attempts to run a boarding house fell to earth along with a tenant who slipped on a broken staircase. This resulted in a lawsuit and Morry lost his shirt. Morry became depressed and Suze began to focus on her spiritual side.

Suze then had to support herself and turned to waitressing where she could earn up to $400 a week.
She borrowed $52,000 to invest through a representative at Merrill Lynch Wealth Management. She lost it all but later trained as an account executive at Merrill Lynch. She worked extremely hard and being flexible she managed to change her story and now runs a company that generates over $40 million a year. She is now an American author, a leading financial advisor, motivational speaker and television host.

The story she sells about how she created her fortune is the holistic blending of financial wisdom with the appeal of higher level of consciousness and emotion. Often at seminars, she'll hold up a dollar bill and refer to the seal, i.e. the eye surrounded by rays of light and enclosed by a triangle (at the tip of the pyramid). Her interpretation is that, "The eye represents spirituality, the third eye, and there's an aspect of money that is very emotional and spiritual. It's on a one dollar bill because we need to be one with our money".

To be an object of fascination you must have a rich and complex personal story. Who you are, where you come from and what makes you tick. At this point people often say, "Nobody is really interested in my life, so how can I possibly create a rich and complex story?" Well you would be surprised; it's just a question of digging a little deeper and pulling out the information. Start at the beginning to uncover your dynamic stories. Use a series of building blocks, one at a time, to gradually uncover the detail from the very beginning and stack more information to create a meaningful structure, i.e. consider where you come from: What is your heritage? What has happened to you in life? What are the turning points and influences?

Step-by-step process for developing your personal story

Exercise:

Personal stories are built from the raw materials of life experiences as explained above. Let's now turn to an exercise to enable you to develop your own personal story.

(i) Given below are some broad headings and examples that you can relate to your past. Identify at least three things about your past that might be useful in developing a story using these idea generators:

Ethnicity or nationality:
Common, national or cultural traditions
Family Members:
Parents: father, mother, stepfather, stepmother
Other family: siblings, grandfather, grandmother, uncles, aunts etc.
Childhood: discoveries, strategies, place, memories
Obstacles/Turning Points: stuttering problem, no college education, car/home being repossessed, bankruptcy, changes in health (e.g. diabetes), change of partner, husband or wife
Persons of influence: teachers, guardians, club leaders, coaches.

(ii) Now list out at least 30 story starters from the above ideas. This can be done fairly quickly as a brainstorm – note down those thoughts that come to you quickly.

(iii) From that list identify and focus on 3 key areas that strongly resonate with you to create a story about yourself.

To help you further I'll refer back to the personal story I gave in the introduction when I spoke of my childhood and my parents:

"My own personal story was shaped from the age of seven. It was discovered that I was dyslexic; ironically not just a difficult word to pronounce, but also to try and spell! In addition to this my parents struggled financially and found it difficult to make ends meet. Mum made my clothes and cut my hair using the stylish 'basin cut' method. Birthday and Christmas presents were homemade. As an adult now I understand and appreciate the efforts that were made, but as a kid at the time I really wanted what other kids had, the bionic 'Six Million Dollar Man' action figure".

Although this is just a paragraph that forms a small block of a story, it can be fitting when it's used appropriately. It does actually contain a number of poignant remarks which are likely to strike a similar chord with the reader. These are points that may resonate in others, points that other people can associate with and relate to by drawing upon similar memories and experiences:
- Being diagnosed with a life changing condition at a very young age.
- Financial instability and hardship within the family.
- To really want something, but circumstances would just not allow it.

So now you have the idea and are ready to complete the exercise. It may take a little time to gather together the story blocks and you may recall memories you had seemingly forgotten, but I can assure you that this will be a good investment of your time. It's an opportunity to bring to light information that will grow into a rich, dynamic and complex web or catalogue of stories that can then be applied and adapted to suit many varied situations in the future.

Your philosophy in life

When designing a story we think about structure, what we're going to say and why we're going to say it. However, it is particularly important to know your intended outcome and people often struggle to understand and decide what this should be. The answer is surprisingly quite straightforward; it is to decide *what you stand for.*

When designing an influential story, your philosophy on life and what you stand for will shine through.
A dictionary definition of *philosophy* states, "A theory or attitude that acts as a guiding principle for behaviour".

One of my personal philosophies in life is, "Always work hard, do your best and you will succeed". We all have different philosophies that can relate to different aspects of our lives and therefore any stories we choose to tell will often be contextual. It can sometimes be difficult to ascertain what that philosophy may be, but the following exercise should help.

Exercise:

It is worthwhile considering and unpacking a philosophy linked to a particular area of your life to provide clarity and to form the basis of a story we want to tell.

Consider and create a concise statement that you believe reflects your personal philosophy for each of the subjects listed below. Let's take a quick example first with regard to money:
"Spend a little, save a little". Or "Look after the pennies and the pounds will look after themselves".

Consider the following list and what you think your philosophy might be in relation to each:

Family, therapy, play, money, business, success, sales, time, religion, spiritual, politics, health and fitness.

Once you have noted your philosophy for each area, just reflect on it for a moment to fully appreciate what that actually means. In the examples for money I have given above, the philosophy tends to relate to the importance of saving, avoiding debt and hardship; ensuring you have sufficient funds to draw upon when needed. This seems to be a sensible philosophy and one that people can relate to.

Memorable stories.

What are the elements of a story that will stay with you? What will you retain and remember that creates change? Would these be key facts, a message being taught or something in the storyline?

Let's turn our attention to a fascinating book by the brothers Chip and Dan Heath called *Made to Stick - Why some ideas take hold and others come unstuck.* Their research looked into how we get people to act on ideas. They refer to the importance of telling stories and provide 6 principles of a successful idea to ensure it becomes *'sticky'*, i.e. remembered and changes something. Apparently you don't need all 6 to have a sticky idea, but the more the better. Briefly they span:

Simple – prioritise your ideas and stick to the core of any idea.
Unexpected – grab people's attention by surprising them. Violate expectations. Generate interest and curiosity.
Concrete – Ensure an idea can be grasped and remembered later.
Credible – Make the idea believable. Let people test your ideas for themselves.
Emotional – Help people see the importance of an idea and let them feel something.
Storie**s** – Empower people to use an idea through narrative. Tell stories. Hearing stories acts a sort of mental flight simulator preparing us to respond more quickly and effectively.

This then provides the acronym for **S.U.C.C.E.S.s**. and is a powerful tool for selling an idea in many areas of life, including business.

Sceptics amongst us may be thinking, "Does this sticky stuff really work?" To prove the point that it does, and very effectively, I will quickly relay the story the Heath brothers use as an example in the book about the urban legend known as 'The Kidney Heist'. There are various versions in circulation as it has been passed from a friend to a friend, but broadly:

A business traveller had some time to kill before his flight and went to a local bar for a drink. He finished his drink and an attractive woman offered to buy him another. She returned with drinks for them both and the businessman took a sip. That was the last thing he remembered until he woke up, disoriented, lying in a hotel bathtub, his body submerged in ice. Trying to figure out where he was he spotted a note that said, "Don't move, call 911". A cell phone rested on a small table beside the bathtub. He picked it up and called 911, his fingers numb and clumsy from the ice. The operator seemed oddly familiar with his situation. She said, "Sir, I want you to reach behind you, slowly and carefully. Is there a tube protruding from your lower back?" Anxious, he felt around behind him. Sure enough, there was a tube. The operator said, "Sir, don't panic, but one of your kidneys has been harvested. There's a ring of organ thieves operating in this city, and they got to you. Paramedics are on their way. Don't move until they arrive".

Just imagine that you have closed the book right now, taken an hour long break and then called a friend to tell them the story without rereading it. There's a very high probability that you could tell it almost perfectly with all the important information. This story 'sticks' because we understand it, we remember it, and we can retell it later. If we believe that it might be true, it might change our behaviour permanently.   Now then, here's the thing…… from now on, would you readily accept a drink from attractive stranger in a bar?

The story is influential, but it is only a legend. This brings to mind a wonderful quote by Mark Twain (American writer, entrepreneur, publisher, and lecturer, 1835-1910): *"A lie can get halfway around the world before the truth can even get its boots on."*

I have previously mentioned the tale of *Robin Hood* and no doubt you'll also be familiar with this particular legend. So what do you remember about him: What's his real name? What was the king's name at the time? What type of life did he lead before he became Robin Hood? In what year was it set? Unless you're familiar with the story of Robin Hood the facts are not likely to 'stick' and the story may not be transformative. But one thing I can immediately recall, 'Robin Hood stole from the rich to give to the poor', and this is due to the nature of the storytelling and what was taught.

Now what do I recall about Richard Adams' *Watership Down'?* Well, it was set in an idyllic rural landscape in England's Downs - a stirring tale of adventure, courage and survival that followed a band of very special creatures on their flight from the intrusion of man and the certain destruction of their home. Immediately I recall it was in fact about the harrowing times facing a group of brave rabbits.

In Stephen Covey's top-selling business and self-help book *The 7 Habits of Highly Effective People*, what are the seven lessons? Now assuming that you have read the book, what do you remember from it? I'm guessing it's one of the stories? The one that was most prominent in my mind was the story he tells about when he and his wife were struggling with one of his sons. His son was having a very difficult time at school and was underperforming academically. Socially the son was considered was immature and embarrassing to those closest to him. They did everything possible to help him as parents to ensure he was successful. They tried to psych him up using positive mental attitude techniques but the efforts adversely impacted on his self-esteem. From the personal information I have previously disclosed, you'll known that I suffered similar problems during childhood. You can see how I readily relate to, and empathise with, this story - that's why it has stuck with me.

Recapping the plot so far.

What have we learned in this chapter?

We have been collecting the parts to build our story. We have collected the elements of a storyline and how to turn these into a sequence to arouse specific emotions by considering the building blocks. We have looked at story events; an experience, an encounter and conversations that have all contributed to creating a meaningful change in that situation. These were expressed in terms of values and benefits to the listener.

We have explored many such events earlier in the book and you can see how it's possible to cast your stories, using the various frameworks provided, to allow you to build the blocks and allow a fascinating story to unfold. For example, *The Hero's Journey* is a template that can be used to write a story to encourage someone to respond to conflict, overcome adversity and be influenced by a discovery or an intervention from a mentor/coach/wise person.

You now have a range of tools to use to allow you to start to create your own catalogue of stories, but let's not forget the importance of the ultimate story purpose.

In this book we're not suggesting that you write stories to entertain people. Yes that can be a separate benefit, but primarily our intention is to have impact and therefore the story must have a purpose. You will therefore need to carefully consider which of your stories you would use to suit the purpose and context of the situation being faced. If you realise your story has no real purpose, no matter how much you love it, then put it to one side and find one that does.

We have covered some meaningful story purposes in this chapter:

*To introduce yourself, who you are, i.e. this will be a form of personal or even corporate branding

*To gain authority, why you're here and why somebody should listen to you

* To create empathy. We are all alike; sharing similar experiences creates a bond

* To make us human makes us believable and trustworthy

* To deliver difficult information

* To introduce your philosophy, your work ethics or even a mindset

* To create a value or a belief. To have your team of people follow these and engage with you as a manager or entrepreneur

* Together with your team, peer colleagues or even senior colleagues, help to build a collective self-confidence and courage to create action

* The importance of stories being 'sticky'. What do you now remember about the story of the 'Kidney Heist'?

Much of the above takes an inward look to create personal stories relevant to the individual. In the next chapter we will broaden out this concept to consider preparing stories *for others* - whether it is for individuals or groups of people, it's important to achieve impact.

CHAPTER 6

STORIES FOR OTHER PEOPLE.
- ALWAYS KNOW THE CORE PURPOSE.

Now we have discovered how to access a rich treasure trove of stories from our own lives, let's turn our attention to designing stories for other people.

When designing a story for your team or for an individual, there are some fundamental points to bear in mind: Is storytelling the best medium for the message? What is the goal? How can you measure success?

Determine the goal and keep to the core purpose.

Having beaten the drum about the wonders of storytelling it may seem odd at this stage, but it's important to check and verify if storytelling is the most appropriate medium to deliver a message. In order to determine this, we need to expend some initial hard work and effort to elicit key information to consider if telling a story for the subject would be effective. There is an initial investment of time, but this period of preparation is critical in discovering and obtaining optimum information to improve your chances of success with storytelling.

It's possible your subject may come to you with a disjointed wish list of demands in the expectation you can respond with a story:

- A direct response is sought about how to do something or address a particular issue.
- You may be given specific data to use, which may be quite irrelevant.
- Somebody may be pressing you for the facts associated with a problem.
- You may be approached for some advice or guidance on a matter and perhaps which books to read.
- You may be told what the subject thinks you should do and this may be highly inappropriate.

You can therefore see that although your subject or audience is well meaning and have the best intentions at heart, they may not be truly focused on the right issue. Their remarks could be misleading and cause you to veer off at a tangent. Having that correct focus isn't always easy and that's because of one simple issue. When most people communicate they often have no specific *goal* in mind. In the absence of any clear goal, it doesn't matter what skills or techniques you use, you are likely to fail.

We all know people who tend to ramble and never get to the point. It can be entertaining when chatting with a group of friends, but it will have no value if there is no outcome to the communication. Whether you are a therapist, a manager, a leader, an entrepreneur or just a friend, it makes sense to ensure that the stories you tell have a key purpose at their core.

When designing a story our first question becomes, "What is the goal?" It may be all well and good to have a goal, but can this then be stated succinctly? For example, during my training courses I often tell the story of my young son having a temper tantrum because I will not buy him an ice cream. He throws himself to the ground in a very public place on a busy afternoon. In itself this may not be unusual or interesting unless it's your child. However, the purpose of this story is to take a concept and hopefully illustrate it in an entertaining way using a clear goal. The goal here is to introduce the idea that, "the person or thing with the most flexibility will control the outcome" (known as *The Requisite Law of Variety* taken from the field of Cybernetics). I don't want such a public display of this behaviour and my son must learn respect.

Having stated the goal, the audience then has the expectation that the story will lead somewhere. Furthermore, this example is not an uncommon experience and is likely to be recognised universally with other parents or guardians. As described in the previous chapter, this topic is likely to resonate with others and create empathy and understanding leading to a connection with the storyteller, i.e. it becomes relevant to the person hearing it as well as the person telling it.

In this story I explain at length how I also drop to the ground and sit alongside my son to exhibit the same behaviour amidst the swarming crowds. I am demonstrating the flexibility required in order to try and control that outcome. We simply sit together and time stands still. After a while my son declares, "I don't want an ice cream any more". He jumps up, I join him and we walk off together. The goal has been achieved.

I tell many stories in my classes and they all connect to a purpose to aid understanding and learning.

Know your audience.

The story above may have a broad appeal, but it's important to be clear that your audience must have some interest and understanding in the topic in order for your story to achieve impact. It's worth reiterating here a point I made in Chapter 2. I once knew of a friend who was passionate about every aspect of football. It didn't matter if it was the typical British sport, or American Soccer, he could tell endless stories with detailed facts and figures. Unfortunately he assumed everybody else liked football as much as he did and so he would relate his stories endlessly. Often his audience would have no interest in this subject and they would just switch off and their eyes glaze over.

It's always important to know the interests of your audience and target your stories accordingly. To demonstrate this point further, I want to take the example of when I was invited to speak at a corporate conference in front of the top tiers of senior managers. This was a rather plush event and the delegates were all smartly groomed and attired in dark suits, refined ties and crisp white shirts/blouses. I was one of a number of speakers and I was scheduled to speak first, however, another speaker approached me to ask if I would mind if he went first. He said he had a new story that would suit the situation well and that it would lead nicely into my introduction. Now regrettably, and rather naively, I accepted his request and off he went on stage.

His story began with 'Once upon a time' and lapsed into anecdotes about 'fluffy clouds' and 'rabbits'. I was able to appreciate how this chap was trying to deliver his message, but sadly it was wholly inappropriate for this particular group of people and they quickly became disengaged. He concluded to receive a hesitant ripple of applause…..and then he introduced me. Unfortunately he had set the scene quite poorly and had given a low expectation for the standard of speakers to follow. No pressure then! Fortunately I had prepared well. I knew the company, I knew the audience and I was aware of the expectation. I had researched and was fully prepared to deliver a story with impact, fascination and credibility. This was a story about leadership and authority.

My speaking slot went exceedingly well and I managed to set a new standard that captivated the audience and set a new tone for the subsequent speakers to follow. My story was highly *relevant* and I'll explain further how this underpins the power of storytelling.

Relevance.

A successful story therefore hinges on its relevance and so the key issue becomes how to design the content to ensure it would be appropriate for your intended person, people or group, i.e. your audience. This does require an investment of your time as you dive into understanding the values, beliefs and interests of your audience as these will inform the design of the story.

This approach to eliciting the key information about someone has been given various terms by different specialisms over the years, but essentially the processes are similar as they all address some form of profiling. In marketing it is often referred to as 'creating a persona' and in therapy it relates to gathering in depth background knowledge to form a 'psychotherapy case study'.

The information to collect about the individual (or a group) can be quite varied and it's worth trying to ascertain as much of the following as possible:

- Name, job title/occupation
- Physical work location
- Details of role and responsibility
- General demographic make-up: i.e. age, race, ethnicity, gender, salary, education and family etc.
- Goals and challenges: i.e. the focus of the story
- Three or four values that truly matter
- What they believe to be true about the situation
- What do they fear most?
- What is their general attitude to life and/or work?

- What does this person need to know about another person in order to accept them as being trustworthy?
- What is causing this person to be in pain?
- What would be one key thing of significance that could happen to them in the future?
- How would they describe themselves and just how accurate would they consider that to be?

This list isn't exhaustive, but it's a good starting point. In isolation these pieces of information may not seem entirely relevant, but when you consider these together with the purpose and goal of the story they start to take on a greater meaning.

Let's put this into some context by combining the above elements into a short story:

Amira is a young Pakistani woman working for a local London council and is committed to supporting the deprived local community. As part of middle management she is responsible for a team of four people to oversee, monitor and report on corporate projects designed to improve community cohesion and social inclusion. Although she is of Pakistani origin, she has comparatively modern western beliefs and values. Her ultimate ambition is to work for herself and to move to live in Pakistan to help support, educate and develop disadvantaged young people. She is quite spiritual and passionately believes in fate and helping others to achieve their true potential. She will often put the interests of others before her own. She rarely sees this, but sometimes realises this quality has proven detrimental in achieving personal dreams and aspirations.

Her family are very traditional, but Amira has a more modern perspective of equality and sees her future quite differently from the expectations of her family. She currently lives with her parents, but sadly their health is failing and this has created quite a dilemma for her future plans. Amira has two brothers, both married and raising their own families. Recent hospital trips have been upsetting for Amira as her father's health continues to deteriorate and this creates tension and turmoil for longer term caring roles within the family. Previous family attempts for an arranged marriage have not gone well so far and yet Amira expects to marry one day for love, but current circumstances preclude her from living an active social life and meeting people. Nonetheless, she still regularly visualises being in a classroom in Pakistan and teaching young students to help provide an education to improve their future prospects.

Hopefully you can see the wealth of information that had to be carefully gathered on Amira and how it was compiled to make for a fascinating story. I can only reiterate that the preparation in pulling together all the key information is where much of the hard work is concentrated.

"By failing to prepare, you are preparing to fail." Benjamin Franklin, one of the Founding Fathers of the USA (1706–1790).

Once you have the detail you can then begin to design a story. You will now be able to see the relevance of the early chapters of this book and how you can utilise the different models and frameworks to create stories to suit different situations.

Let's relate back to a few of those frameworks we have mentioned to see how they might be applied in particular situations.

(a) Isomorphic Metaphor.

We know that a *metaphor* is regarded as being representative or symbolic of something else. The prefix of *isomorphic* simply means 'corresponding' or 'similar' in form and relations between two groups, i.e. they share the same structure. So it becomes possible to construct a metaphorical story that has the same key elements, events and subjects based on a real life situation. The isomorphic metaphor therefore parallels a situation and this is often the storytelling method most used within therapeutic situations. This is sensible as you will want your clients to associate with the story and to easily pick up its morals and the learnings.

Let's take a hypothetical situation where you are the manager of a team of people and one of your team colleagues feels stuck in their job and unable to progress. As the manager you can see their potential to do so much more, but you are aware that they lack the self-confidence and self-belief to take action to consider new roles to gain greater experience and knowledge. No matter how many times you try to encourage your colleague with interesting new projects and praise them for their hard work, they still do not show the motivation to progress.

You could now start to design a story using the isomorphic metaphor model. It would be possible to create a similar character with the same issues in a different organisation; someone who desperately wants to progress to become a manager themselves with greater responsibility. To be able to meet the requirements of such a responsible role, the typical job specification states that experience of staff supervision and managing finances were essential. The story could then explain how this team member suddenly heard of an opportunity to work in the voluntary sector for a local charity; a role that required some basic experience, but that training would be given help directly supervise two team members and manage the office accommodation budget.

This was recognised as a chance to try something new and gain important experience and transferable skills. The person successfully applied and has just completed their 6 month probation period. They enjoy their new job and their confidence is beginning to soar as the team has been recognised for an award. This demonstrable experience could now be added to their CV in readiness to apply for greater roles in the future in any work sector.

You can see how it is possible to build a story around a basic skeleton framework to convey meaning and purpose to encourage someone to move in a particular direction.

Isomorphic metaphors can be even more effective when used in teaching children. If you want a child to put in the time to work hard, learn and ensure that those efforts would be worthwhile in sustaining a positive outcome over a prolonged period of time; look no further than the story of *The Three Little Pigs* (explained back in Chapter 1). As a reminder, three little pigs built their houses of varying materials. The first was pig was rather lazy and just used simple straw, the second made a little more effort and used sticks, but the third put in the hard work to build a house of study bricks that conformed to all the latest building regulations; it was able to withstand an attack by the Big Bad Wolf and the pig survived. The moral being; put in the hard work upfront and you will live to benefit from the rewards.

(b) The Hero's Journey

This is the framework that can be most effectively applied to write a bestselling book or produce a blockbuster movie. It is used to design stories that inspire, change and motivate.

It can be used in many circumstances, most notably:

- *Keynote speeches*: Often used to establish an important and main underlying theme in a corporate or commercial setting.
- *Motivational speakers:* Intended to motivate, inspire, change or transform an audience.
- *Team Talk*: To relay an important message to team colleagues. Often used to unite the group and inspire them to strive to achieve a particular common objective or outcome.
- *Transformational work*: More in-depth therapeutic work to achieve an outcome over a period of time.

Let's take an example of organisational change impacting on a team of people. This is likely to be a common theme as many companies undergo reorganisation and change in order to survive and thrive. However, fundamental change of this kind is often met with initial resistance and is often seen as a threat. So you have the opportunity to apply the framework for *The Hero's Journey* to design a story that tracks progress of the situation through to a successful conclusion. The successive stages of your story can be adapted and applied in similar situations in the future as they tend to follow the same format (full details given in Chapter 3).

(i) Hearing A Calling:
A strong urge towards a particular way of life.

A new Chief Executive has been appointed to introduce radical organisational change and new strategies to improve performance and productivity. There needed to be fundamental changes to the organisational structure to ensure efficiency savings. Employees would be expected to apply and compete for new posts in the new structure and there is the possibility of displaced staff and redundancy.

Jenny worked as a middle manager in Human Resources and was well aware of the company's past extravagances that often drew media attention. She could see the need for review if the company was going to be successful in the future, but she felt vulnerable and the prospect of losing her job would have dire consequences for her young family.

(ii) Accepting The Calling:
The situation escalates, possibly as a result of external pressures or from something within. An acceptance to face change.

Following a full consultation process with staff, new directorate structures were determined and new job specifications prepared. There was inevitable reluctance from staff faced with such significant change, but all employees were invited to apply and compete for the new posts. Despite repeated attempts by employees to change the structures and delay implementation, time was pressing if the company was to survive and a major appointment process was soon underway.

Jenny became anxious and worried, but realised these were natural emotions in the circumstances. She was heavily involved in the consultation processes and ensured that her views were taken into account. She realised there was certain inevitability about the situation and that there was no option but to accept it and proactively face the challenges ahead.

(iii) Crossing A Threshold:
Likely to be a milestone or an unfamiliar change in direction. A point where The Hero has made a commitment.

The organisation publishes the final structures and makes available all new job specifications for employees to consider. Jenny obtains several of these to study and realised that there was the opportunity to apply for a more senior role, which would represent promotion. She wondered if this was possible and sought advice and guidance from her line manager.

(iv) Finding Your Guardians Or Mentors:
Possibly seasoned travellers, often wise people met along the way that can provide support, advice or guidance for the journey.

Jenny spent much time with her manager who was able to fully explain the restructuring process and that she would certainly have the opportunity to compete for a more senior post in view of her experience, skills and qualifications. Unbeknown to her, she was also eligible for some additional training in interview skills/techniques – useful as she hadn't been interviewed in some time and was a little rusty.

(v) Facing A Challenge:
A point of confrontation – a resistance, something becomes realised, possibly something unknown, perhaps a fear. Often referred to as trials or tests to begin transformation.

Jenny completed and submitted her job application form for the senior position. She soon received an acknowledgment that she had been shortlisted to attend an initial practical assessment and this would in turn determine whether she is invited to final interview. She was aware that there were five other candidates competing for the new job, some older with greater experience. Jenny started to doubt herself and fear crept in. But she realised she had nothing to lose and much to gain. She prepared for the appointment process ahead.

(vi) Transforming Your Demon:
From the confrontation/fear something new is discovered. A new awareness is realised, a growing positivity or a new perspective emerges. The transformation of a demon into a positive resource.

Jenny passed the practical assessment with flying colours and went on to impress the interview panel with her innovative ideas for the future. She was able to turn her fear into focus and was offered the senior role. The rigorous selection process verified that she was capable of doing so much more and that her talents were recognised by others. As her confidence grew, Jenny could see that the major restructuring exercise represented an opportunity and a chance to move forward with her career.

(vii) Completing The Task Called For:
The issue has been tackled and overcome. There is an acknowledgement, a reward or point of celebration.

Jenny was successfully promoted into her new senior managerial position within HR and was able use her abilities to implement new and innovative ways of working in line with the organisations new mission statement. She was now financially more secure and able to pursue a mortgage with her partner.

(viii) Returning Home:
The completion of the adventure and to bring back the reward. The conflict at the beginning has been resolved and the person is transformed to become a hero.

In no time, Jenny was returning to a brand new home and was far better equipped to support her young family. She is seen as something of a hero as her decisions and actions were pivotal in progressing her career and providing greater family stability. She now exudes confidence and is poised and ready to tackle any future challenges that may lie ahead.

You can see how this story transformed Jenny's life. You can also see how the story can be applied to help others facing similar work situations.

(c) Pixar Framework

The Pixar framework, or The Story Spine, was explained in detail in Chapter 4. It is a simple but very effective framework used to deliver a story. It is ideally suited to delivering important messages or to introduce a new idea or concept and here is an example:

Once upon a time there was a young woman called Sophie who wanted to discover and learn more about the art of *storytelling*. She was aware that it was regarded as a powerful method of communication and a way to achieve change and transformation for yourself and others. Sophie worked in a large corporate organisation and wanted to use storytelling techniques to support a change programme. She wanted to learn more but struggled to find a book that comprehensively provided all the key information needed in one convenient place.

Every day
She spoke with colleagues, scoured bookshops and searched the internet for a meaningful book; a reference point that could be regularly used to help develop and utilise various storytelling techniques to achieve positive change within her organisation.

One day
Sophie attended one of John's Storytelling training courses and became transfixed by the various

stories he would tell to exemplify and underline the key learning points. Memorable stories and anecdotes that stuck in her mind to aid her learning and help develop her own skills. She then discovered the existence of John and Stephen's book *'Unlock The Power of Stories- Unlock Potential. Change Your Story, Change Your Life'* and wisely decided to purchase a copy.

Because of that
Sophie was able to read the book from cover to cover to learn and apply the various techniques and frameworks when delivering presentations and speeches throughout her organisation. She found she was able to apply different models in different situations to great effect and everybody found them to be relevant and fascinating.

Because of that (repeated)
The stories had a profound effect on the organisation and staff became more effective, productive and innovative. The company began to thrive and acquire recognised awards in excellence. The more stories she told the more her reputation grew as a change agent.

Until finally
She became prolific at storytelling through practice and determination. Sophie was invited to major presentation circuits to tell the most enthralling stories that would resonate with people's lives. Although she was initially headhunted to work as a senior partner in a highly reputable company, Sophie quickly took the decision to become self-

employed and her company now regularly achieves annual profits in excess of £10m.

And ever since that day *(the missing element from the original Story Spine that can also be used)* Sophie has been grateful to have discovered such a wonderful book that transformed not only her life, but the lives of others. She keeps it with her at all times for ready reference and is ready to tell the next tale to create change.

You can see how the Pixar framework can be quickly applied in almost any situation. In fact, I have successfully used it on one of my websites to tell a story about how my company began in the section 'About us'. It's an important page for any website as it is one of the most visited. Head over to http://www.nlpcourses.com/about-us/ to learn more and consider also how you might like to apply the framework.

Recapping the plot so far.

What have we learned in this chapter?

* Designing meaningful stories takes much time and preparation. Time invested in gathering key information is time well invested and your efforts will be rewarded with positive outcomes.

* Ensure your story has a clear and succinct goal. Adhere to that core purpose throughout and your

audience will have the expectation that the story will lead somewhere.

* Know your audience. Ensure the story content is relevant to them. They must have some interest and understanding in the topic in order for your story to achieve impact.

* Utilise the storytelling frameworks given in the early chapters of this book to best suit the circumstances: e.g. The Isomorphic Metaphor, The Hero's Journey or The Pixar framework.

* Repetition and constantly using examples aids understanding and helps to embed the learning.

The concluding chapter follows and you will be given some simple but effective advice on how to use this book to achieve transformation and success. *Turn the page and turn your life around.*

CHAPTER 7

HOW TO USE THIS BOOK.

You have picked up and carefully read through this book for a reason. Perhaps you have a definite need to embrace change or maybe it's just curiosity or intrigue. In any event, you have been reading a small yet powerful book about communication. Master the skills held within these pages and a world of possibilities will open up for you.

Whether you are an entrepreneur, a manager, a team leader, a salesperson, a therapist, a parent or anyone with a genuine interest in helping others, you now have the opportunity to become a great leader in your field and a highly sought after resource. Surprisingly, there is much commonality within these varied groups of people as they share a similar skills set when engaging with others.

You may have preferred to learn about the structured story frameworks or perhaps you were more intrigued by the way stories can influence and persuade? Either way, you are now equipped with some of the most powerful techniques available to allow you to prepare empowering stories of your own; to help and transform yourself as well as the lives of others.

These are bold promises for such a small book, however, you may now realise that it contains a wealth of information and ideas for you to consider and utilise.

You now have quite a simple a choice. You can actively do something to change lives, or you can put the book on a shelf to gather dust. Just by reading the book will not change the way you communicate – you will have to take what's in the book and do something with it. Remember:

"If you always do what you've always done, you will always get what you've always got".

I have always found this to be an inspirational quote as it reflects a mindset. It's been around for some time and is often attributed to Anthony Robbins, Albert Einstein, Henry Ford, or even Mark Twain. The source doesn't particularly matter, it's the key point it makes. If you want to change what's happening in your life, or the life of another, it's time to tell a new story and change the outcome.

If you are looking for motivation, review the story of *Sophie* in the Pixar example given in Chapter 6. Anything worth doing well in life requires an effort and takes some hard work. Do you remember the hard working third little pig who built his house from bricks and his ultimate reward? If you want to progress from being ordinary to become extraordinary, then you'll need to do that little bit *extra*. Carefully reading this book and actively using some of the frameworks will be worthwhile in achieving a pay-off of success.

I encourage my students to return to undertake my training courses a number of times to embed the learning. I therefore recommend that you read this book at least 3 times. The first time you are likely to assimilate about 20% of the information. The second time you'll think new information has been added, but the content would not have changed – you will have changed. The third time you will own it.

There has been the occasional reference to 'rabbits' throughout the book. Some people might think, "Well if it's good enough for Lewis Carroll, then it's good enough for me". In Carroll's book *Alice in Wonderland* (1865) the white rabbit is often considered to be represented as a transitional symbol and the rabbit hole a metaphor for entry into the unknown. Alice had the most incredible journey and, as a result, she began to change and transform to such a great extent that she remarked:
> *"I can't go back to yesterday - because I was a different person then".*

Towards the end of the story, Alice's transformation was complete and there was no going back. You are now ready to move forward with your life. Start to design stories of your own and be ready to create transformation. You are limited only by your imagination:

"Imagination is more important than knowledge. Knowledge is limited. Imagination encircles the world." Albert Einstein.

Let your imagination run free and start to unlock the power of stories. Beliefs are the stories we tell ourselves. Change your story and change your life.

Unlock The Power Of Stories

Begin a fresh chapter in your life by reflecting and writing those four powerful words - be ready to journey down a new rabbit hole…..

………..*"Once Upon A Time………...."*

Once you've had an opportunity to read the book and to reflect on the content and your learning, John and Stephen would very much appreciate you posting an honest review on Amazon. Just a brief supporting paragraph would allow their storytelling to continue.

BIOGRAPHIES:

JOHN CASSIDY-RICE

John is a highly respected international Master Trainer, NLP Master Practitioner, author and is responsible for a number of businesses. He has worked to support and develop some of the largest and most influential organisations around the world in bringing alive both personal and global transformation.

He lives in a beautiful placed called Chichester, nestled at the foot of the South Downs in West Sussex, England and lives with his partner, children and a greyhound. He is highly creative and known to set himself the most challenging goals; he works hard to achieve these and maintain his high and exacting standards.

He is a highly energetic and engaging speaker and trainer who has had great impact and influence in many countries internationally. John continues to create and build a range of resources on personal and business development and these can be accessed via his website www.NLPcourses.com

Despite a busy working life, John is always pleased to hear from others with their questions, feedback or comments. Even if you want to just say 'Hi' he can be reached by email at john@nlpcourses.com

STEPHEN ENGWELL

Stephen is a Chartered Fellow of the Chartered Institute of Personnel & Development (CIPD) living in England. His extensive career and experience in Human Resources with local government helped to develop his specialism in Learning & Organisational Development.

Stephen met John whilst attending his training courses and became intrigued by 'Neuro Linguistic Programme' (NLP) and Hypnosis. He soon qualified as a Master NLP Practitioner and now has an expanding portfolio career. He works as a Consultant, and an Associate for a number of companies, to help and support others in solving and overcoming their issues and limiting beliefs.

In recent years he has been sought for his writing skills to support authors in creating, developing and writing content material for their books. He was delighted to take the opportunity to work alongside John; to support him in his quest to raise a greater understanding and awareness about the powers of storytelling and how this can unlock potential to positively change people's lives.

APPENDIX

Further information relating to certain quotes given:

During the preparation of this book there was particular interest in certain quotes. To try and minimise any misunderstanding, here are some explanations for the following:

(*) **It is often said that, "With great power comes great responsibility".**

Historically this quote has been attributed to many different people and even the greatest researchers seem unable to trace a definitive source. In contemporary times it can be attributed to a scene from the 2002 superhero film *Spider-Man*, and is a quote said by Benjamin Parker ('Uncle Ben') to Peter Parker (aka Spider-Man) shortly before getting killed by a carjacker. Peter was the son of Ben's brother and his wife, both killed in a plane crash. Ben raised Peter as his own son. The film was based on the Marvel Comics character created by writer Stan Lee and artist Steve Ditko.

However, similar quotes have also been used quite extensively in the past.

In 1906 the statesman Winston Churchill delivered a speech in the House of Commons that included: *"Where there is great power there is great responsibility"*.

In 1908 the 26th President of the USA, Theodore Roosevelt, wrote in a letter to decline a third term as President: *"…..I believe in power; but I believe that responsibility should go with power….."*

In 1945 Franklin D. Roosevelt (32nd President of USA) prepared a speech about Thomas Jefferson (3rd President of USA) that was released by Journalists following Roosevelt's abrupt death: *"Today we have learned in the agony of war that great power involves great responsibility………"*

Some basic research will reveal many other possible sources from much earlier dates, but no one appears to have put it quite so succinctly until it appeared in the Spider-Man Marvel comic book *Amazing Fantasy #15* (1962).

Given the power of storytelling, the point being made in this book is that if you have the ability to do something, make sure that you do it for the good of others. Take your Spidey sense and always use it wisely.

(**) **"The needs of the many outweigh the needs of the one".**

Derivations of this quote are made in various scenes in the Star Trek films, including *Star Trek Into Darkness* (2013). Originally, in a climactic scene towards the end of *The Wrath of Khan* (1982), The Starship USS Enterprise is in imminent danger of destruction and Spock enters a highly radioactive chamber to try and repair the ship's drive to selflessly save the crew. Spock says to Kirk, "Don't grieve, Admiral. It is logical. The needs of the many outweigh ...." Kirk finishes for him, "The needs of the few." Spock replies, "Or the one." Spock perishes and Kirk loses his dear friend.

In the subsequent film *The Search for Spock (1984),* the crew of the Enterprise discovers that Spock's body and soul survived separately and that they could be brought together and combined again. Once restored Spock asks Kirk why the crew had made such extreme efforts to save him. Kirk answers, "Because the needs of the one outweigh the needs of the many." So this is a complete reversal or the flip side of what was said initially in the previous film.

The theme continues again into the next film *The Voyage Home (1986),* when Spock's mother questions him about the same claim and this time some clarity is given. In view of Spock's Vulcan perspective, the film focuses on the issue of *logic* and the Vulcan's perceived understanding of irrational human behaviour.

Just to complicate matters, the quote has resurfaced in the first season of the *Star Trek Discovery* TV show (2017). This series is set a decade before the events of the original Star Trek series, and so arguably this is likely to be the earliest known reference.

In this book, however, the quote has been used to simply try to make the point that there are many different perspectives in all situations of life. What one person sees, another may see quite differently. We are providing you with a number of different storytelling frameworks to allow you to decide what will work best for you in any given situation. One of the basic NLP principles I teach on my training courses is: 'Have sufficient flexibility to be able to keep changing your behaviour until you get your outcome', i.e. if what you're doing isn't working, do something different' (see example in Chapter 6).

You can exercise flexibility when telling stories to discover what approach works best for you. Unlock the power of stories, change your story and change your life.

A

Aesop's Fables, 21
Albert Einstein, 19, 141, 143
Amazon, 17, 18, 143
Annette Simmons, 98
Apple, 16, 17
audience, 16, 31, 49, 50, 51, 78, 98, 102, 120, 121, 122, 123, 124, 130, 138, 139

B

Barack Obama, 12
brain, 11, 27, 28, 29, 30, 38, 66, 73, 74, 86
Brian McDonald, 84, 86
business, 2, 3, 15, 16, 17, 18, 28, 34, 59, 66, 83, 91, 104, 106, 111, 113, 115, 144

C

children, 10, 15, 21, 32, 34, 39, 73, 92, 129, 144
Chip and Dan Heath, 112
CIPD, 23, 144
communication, 3, 11, 16, 26, 27, 29, 34, 38, 40, 41, 66, 120, 136, 140
conflict, 49, 51, 57, 116, 135

D

Daniel Pink, 83
David Bowie, 55
David Gordon, 76, 77, 78, 81, 87
Dennis Haysbert, 12
Dr Roger Sperry, 28
Dr. Giacomo Rizzolatti, 73, 74, 86
dyslexic, 13, 14, 66, 109

E

education, 20, 22, 108, 125, 127
Edward Bulwer-Lytton, 41
ego, 44, 45, 46, 47, 48, 50, 51
Emma Coats, 84
emotions, 28, 116, 132
Employee Engagement, 92
entrepreneur, 99, 102, 105, 114, 118, 120, 140

F

fables, 10
fairy tales, 10
fascination, 98, 99, 100, 101, 107, 123

G

George Lucas, 13, 54
Goal setting, 35
Grimm's Fairy Tales, 21
Guardians, 56, 61, 62, 133

H

hemispheres, 28, 29
Human Resources, 23, 131, 145

I

id, 44, 45, 46, 47, 48, 49, 51
influence, 12, 20, 22, 26, 34, 40, 42, 62, 66, 89, 90, 94, 95, 96, 97, 98, 99, 100, 101, 105, 108, 140, 144
intuition, 29, 39
Isomorphic, 72, 76, 127, 129, 139

J

Jim Rohn, 99
JOHN CASSIDY-RICE, 10, 144
Joseph Campbell, 54, 56, 62, 68, 70

K

King Arthur, 41, 42, 50

L

language, 28, 34, 38, 41, 66, 80, 87, 96
leaders, 12, 28, 74, 87, 108
legends, 10
Les Misérables, 21
Lewis Carroll, 25, 88, 142
linguistic, 94, 96

M

Malcolm Gladwell, 66
Manager, 58, 59, 60, 61, 63, 64, 65, 67, 68
marketing, 3, 16, 17, 27, 31, 40, 124
Matrix, 55, 58, 59, 60, 61, 62, 64, 65, 67, 68, 69
Mentors, 56, 61, 62, 133
Merlin, 41, 42, 50
metaphor, 36, 37, 38, 39, 76, 77, 78, 79, 87, 127, 128, 142
Metaphors, 34, 72, 76
mindset, 100, 118, 141
Mirror Neurons, 3, 9, 72, 73, 74, 86
morals, 21, 33, 34, 45, 91, 128
myths, 10, 15, 54

N

NLP, 24, 66, 76, 80, 81, 87, 144, 145, 149
Nobel Prize, 28, 106
Norman Vincent Peale, 23

O

obstacle, 49, 51, 64

P

persuade, 26, 140
philosophy, 90, 92, 110, 111, 118
Pixar, 3, 9, 13, 72, 73, 83, 84, 85, 135, 138, 139, 141
Professor Brian Cox, 19
public speaker, 27, 106
purpose, 8, 16, 66, 92, 117, 119, 121, 122, 125, 129, 138

R

rabbit, 6, 25, 27, 30, 38, 42, 43, 48, 51, 59, 60, 86, 87, 142, 143
Rabbit – Road – Car, 29
Repetition, 30, 31, 39, 139
Requisite Law of Variety, 121
Richard Adams, 115
Richard Feynman, 19

S

scientific, 6, 18, 19
self-esteem, 14, 45, 115
selling, 16, 37, 38, 51, 83, 101, 113, 115
Shawshank Redemption, 47
Shrek, 55, 58, 59, 61, 62, 63, 65, 67, 68, 69, 70

Sigmund Freud, 24, 41, 43
Simon Sinek, 16
Sir Richard Branson, 14
Star Trek, 75, 147, 148
Star Wars, 4, 13, 46, 54, 55, 58, 59, 60, 62, 63, 64, 67, 68, 69
Stephen Covey, 115
STEPHEN ENGWELL, 10, 144
Stephen Hawkins, 19
stories, 3, 4, 5, 6, 10, 11, 12, 13, 15, 16, 17, 18, 19, 21, 24, 27, 29, 30, 32, 33, 37, 39, 40, 42, 43, 48, 50, 51, 53, 55, 70, 72, 74, 83, 86, 87, 89, 90, 94, 98, 101, 103, 104, 105, 107, 108, 110, 112, 115, 116, 117, 118, 119, 121, 122, 123, 127, 130, 136, 137, 138, 140, 142, 143, 149
story, 2, 5, 11, 12, 13, 14, 15, 16, 17, 18, 19, 20, 21, 22, 23, 24, 29, 30, 31, 32, 33, 34, 35, 36, 39, 41, 42, 43, 45, 46, 47, 48, 49, 50, 51, 53, 55, 66, 69, 70, 74, 75, 76, 77, 78, 79, 80, 81, 82, 84, 86, 87, 90, 96, 97, 98, 99, 100, 101, 104, 105, 106, 107, 108, 109, 110, 111, 112, 113, 114, 115, 116, 117, 118, 119, 120, 121, 122, 123, 124, 125, 127, 128, 129, 131, 135, 138, 139, 140, 141, 142, 143, 149
Story Spine', 84
storyteller, 4, 13, 19, 44, 99, 121
storytelling, 2, 3, 4, 10, 12, 13, 15, 24, 26, 27, 28, 29, 31, 32, 33, 34, 36, 38, 39, 40, 41, 46, 51, 53, 54, 70, 71, 72, 74, 75, 81, 83, 84, 86, 87, 89, 90, 91, 97, 98, 105, 115, 119, 124, 128, 136, 137, 139, 143, 145, 147, 149
Sun Tzu, 37
superego, 44, 46, 47, 48, 49, 51
Suze Orman, 106

T

teacher, 20, 21, 27, 84
Ted Talks, 16
THE HERO'S JOURNEY, 9, 20, 53, 54, 55, 56, 68, 71, 75, 116, 131, 139
Therapist, 57, 58, 59, 60, 61, 63, 64, 65, 67, 68
therapy, 51, 77, 80, 93, 111, 124
Three Little Pigs, 23, 130
transformational, 49

U

university study, 19

V

Victor Hugo, 21

W

Winston Churchill, 85, 146

Z

Zappos, 18

Printed in Poland
by Amazon Fulfillment
Poland Sp. z o.o., Wrocław